The Seafarers THE ATLANTIC CROSSING

TIME
LIFE ®
BOOKS

Other Publications:

The Cover: Towed by a steam-powered
tugboat, a packet ship leaves a Belfast
quay for the passage to America, as an
　　　d vessel approaches under full sail.
　　　　ears during the second half
　　　　　Century, such ships transported
　　　　　,000 emigrants westward
　　　　　tic, returning with cargoes
　　　　　ɔbacco and timber.

　　　　　identified the packet
　　　　　ll Line. Established in
　　　　　e first of more
　　　　　to put Atlantic shipping
　　　　　nd schedule.

The Seafarers

THE ATLANTIC CROSSING

by Melvin Maddocks

AND THE EDITORS OF TIME-LIFE BOOKS

TIME-LIFE BOOKS, ALEXANDRIA, VIRGINIA

Time-Life Books Inc.
is a wholly owned subsidiary of
TIME INCORPORATED

FOUNDER: Henry R. Luce 1898-1967

Editor-in-Chief: Henry Anatole Grunwald
President: J. Richard Munro
Chairman of the Board: Ralph P. Davidson
Executive Vice President: Clifford J. Grum
Chairman, Executive Committee: James R. Shepley
Editorial Director: Ralph Graves
Group Vice President, Books: Joan D. Manley
Vice Chairman: Arthur Temple

TIME-LIFE BOOKS INC.

MANAGING EDITOR: Jerry Korn
Executive Editor: David Maness
Assistant Managing Editors: Dale M. Brown (planning),
George Constable, Thomas H. Flaherty Jr. (acting),
Martin Mann, John Paul Porter
Art Director: Tom Suzuki
Chief of Research: David L. Harrison
Director of Photography: Robert G. Mason
Assistant Art Director: Arnold C. Holeywell
Assistant Chief of Research: Carolyn L. Sackett
Assistant Director of Photography: Dolores A. Littles

CHAIRMAN: John D. McSweeney
President: Carl G. Jaeger
Executive Vice Presidents: John Steven Maxwell,
David J. Walsh
Vice Presidents: George Artandi (comptroller);
Stephen L. Bair (legal counsel); Peter G. Barnes;
Nicholas Benton (public relations); John L. Canova;
Beatrice T. Dobie (personnel); Carol Flaumenhaft
(consumer affairs); James L. Mercer (Europe/South
Pacific); Herbert Sorkin (production); Paul R. Stewart (marketing)

The Seafarers

Editorial Staff for *The Atlantic Crossing:*
Editor: Anne Horan
Designer: Herbert H. Quarmby
Picture Editor: John Conrad Weiser
Text Editors: Bobbie Conlan, Lydia Preston
Staff Writers: Carol Dana, Stuart Gannes, Lee Greene,
Fran Moshos
Researchers: Patti H. Cass, Philip Brandt George,
Barbara Brownell, Therese A. Daubner, Roxie France,
Adrienne George, Sheila M. Green, Susan Kelly,
Ann Dusel Kuhns, Anne Muñoz-Furlong
Art Assistants: Michelle René Clay, Robert K. Herndon
Editorial Assistant: Ellen Keir

Special Contributors
Frederick King Poole, Harold C. Field,
Edward P. H. Kern, David S. Thomson (text); Martha
Reichard George, Barbara Hicks (research)

Editorial Production
Production Editor: Douglas B. Graham
Operations Manager: Gennaro C. Esposito,
Gordon E. Buck (assistant)
Assistant Production Editor: Feliciano Madrid
Quality Control: Robert L. Young (director), James J. Cox
(assistant), Daniel J. McSweeney, Michael G. Wight (associates)
Art Coordinator: Anne B. Landry
Copy Staff: Susan B. Galloway (chief), Anne T. Connell,
Victoria Lee, Celia Beattie
Picture Department: Jane A. Martin
Traffic: Kimberly K. Lewis

Correspondents: Elisabeth Kraemer (Bonn);
Margot Hapgood, Dorothy Bacon, Lesley Coleman
(London); Susan Jonas, Lucy T. Voulgaris (New York);
Maria Vincenza Aloisi, Josephine du Brusle (Paris);
̄ Natanson (Rome).
̄ assistance was provided by Nakanori Tashiro,
̄ kyo. The editors also wish to thank: Helga
̄ ̄armer (Boston); Kathy Nolan
̄ ̄uyn (Copenhagen); Judy
̄ ̄llicent Trowbridge
̄ ̄am Hsia, Christina
̄ ̄ Hirschkoff (Paris);
̄ ̄cisco); Dick
̄ ̄audl Lessing (Vienna).

The Author:
Melvin Maddocks has a personal link with Atlantic sailings; his father was a ship chandler in Boston during the latter part of the packet era and witnessed the transition from sail to steam. A columnist and critic for the *Christian Science Monitor,* Maddocks is also a contributor to *Time* and other magazines and the author of *The Great Liners* in the Seafarers series.

The Consultants:
John Horace Parry, Gardiner Professor of Oceanic History and Affairs at Harvard, obtained his Ph.D. from Cambridge University. He is the author of many books on seafaring, among them *The Discovery of the Sea* and *Trade and Dominion.*

John Haskell Kemble, professor emeritus at Pomona College, taught maritime history at that institution for 41 years. He serves as a member of the Secretary of the Navy's Advisory Committee on Naval History.

Cedric Ridgely-Nevitt is Professor of Naval Architecture at the Webb Institute of Naval Architecture in Glen Cove, New York, and is also the author of *American Steamships on the Atlantic.*

Michael K. Stammers is Keeper of Maritime History at Merseyside County Museums in England, and a consultant for BBC radio programs on British seafarers.

Norman J. Brouwer is a marine historian at the South Street Seaport Museum in New York and has advanced degrees from Maine Maritime Academy and the State University of New York.

William Avery Baker, curator of the Hart Nautical Museum at the Massachusetts Institute of Technology, is a naval architect and engineer. He designed the *Mayflower II,* which in 1957 retraced the path of the original *Mayflower* from Plymouth, England, to Plymouth, Massachusetts.

For information about any Time-Life book, please write: Reader Information, Time-Life Books,
541 North Fairbanks Court, Chicago, Illinois 60611.

TIME-LIFE is a trademark of Time Incorporated U.S.A.

Library of Congress Cataloguing in Publication Data
Maddocks, Melvin.
   The Atlantic crossing.
   (The Seafarers)
   Bibliography: p.
   Includes index.
   1. Shipping—United States—History.   2. Navigation—United States—History.   3. United States—Commerce—History   4. United States—History.
I. Time-Life Books. II. Title. III. Series: Seafarers.
HE745.M338   387.5'0973   80-26891
ISBN 0-8094-2726-5
ISBN 0-8094-2727-3 (lib. bdg.)
ISBN 0-8094-2728-1 (retail ed.)

Contents

Chapter 1

Pioneering sails on a trackless sea

 n the gray early-morning hours of July 22, 1620, a group of 35 English Protestants, all of whom had spent nearly 12 years in voluntary exile as Separatists from the Church of England, assembled on the dock of the small port of Delftshaven in the Netherlands. They had just concluded two days of devotions; now they climbed aboard a 60-ton three-master, the *Speedwell*, which stood ready to set sail for Southampton, England. There, 80 fellow travelers were waiting to board a larger, three-masted vessel, the *Mayflower*, and plans called for the two ships to sail in company west across the Atlantic.

On the deck of the *Speedwell*, the travelers were joined by their pastor, the Reverend John Robinson, and other Separatists who had come to see them off. All at once, "sighs and sobs did sound amongst them," wrote William Bradford, one of the leaders. They fell to their knees "with most fervent prayers," he added. "And then with mutual embraces and many tears they took their leaves one of another." The *Speedwell* moved away from the dock, and the passengers raised muskets and fired a volley in salute to those who remained behind. Then, as the wind caught the sails, the passengers grew silent and their thoughts turned to God. "They knew they were pilgrims," Bradford wrote. And so they have been called ever since.

The voyagers had good reason for the trepidations that provoked their sobs and for the prayers that buttressed their hopes. In the early 17th Century the North Atlantic remained a forbidding and mysterious realm, dreaded for its abrupt changes of weather and believed by some sailors to be populated with ship-devouring sea monsters. Occasional vessels did, in fact, disappear so suddenly that they seemed to have been swallowed whole. In 1583 the English navigator Sir Humphrey Gilbert had commanded an expedition of 260 men to Newfoundland, which he claimed in the name of Queen Elizabeth. It was England's first overseas territory, and Gilbert hoped to colonize the site after obtaining more supplies from home. But when he embarked on his pinnace, the *Squirrel*, and sailed back toward England with his small fleet, disaster struck. On a stormy night in midocean, a sailor on an accompanying vessel reported, the lights on the *Squirrel* went out and the ship vanished, never to be seen again.

Other expeditions suffered more protracted adversities. Only two years before the Pilgrims set out, a vessel bound for Virginia had been

On the deck of the 60-ton Speedwell, pioneering emigrants pray for divine assistance as they depart from Holland to rendezvous with the Mayflower in Southampton, England, in 1620. The Speedwell was to have accompanied the Mayflower on the voyage that brought the Pilgrims to North America, but proved too unseaworthy to make the trip.

blown so far off course by a gale that she took six months to reach her destination; 150 of the 200 or so prospective colonists aboard starved at sea. And for those who survived the ocean crossing there awaited the uncertain prospects of life in a forested wilderness whose inhabitants, more often than not, regarded the newcomers with a malevolent eye.

Colonization had not even been a consideration for the intrepid men who had first crossed the Atlantic in the 15th Century: They sought a short, westward route to the spice-rich Orient. Although their notions of geography proved ill-founded, the New World offered great wealth in its own right. Columbus, who made four voyages from Spain between 1492 and 1504, managed to plant a trading post on Hispaniola (now Haiti and the Dominican Republic); out of that small beginning, Spain built an empire in Central and South America that would feed prodigious quantities of gold and silver into its treasury in the century to come. In 1497 John Cabot, sailing under the English flag, landed on the American coast far to the north, probably at Newfoundland; he found no precious metals, but he noted vast amounts of codfish—a staple of the European diet. Soon English, French, Portuguese and Spanish fishermen were hauling tons of codfish from the Grand Banks of Newfoundland and the waters to the south for transport back across the ocean.

Since then, fishing sites, trading posts and settlements of various degrees of durability had sprung up between Quebec and Florida, and to the lures of gold and codfish had been added furs (in great demand by Europe's gentlemen for felt hats and the trimmings on their coats), timber and tobacco. Eventually tobacco would be prized in Europe above every other colonial product.

The men and women who gathered aboard the *Speedwell* that morning in 1620 were keenly aware of the commercial promise of the New World. To be sure, they had initially exiled themselves from England over religious quarrels; contrary to the tenets of the established church, they felt that every congregation should have the right to choose its own pastor, discipline its own members and control the actions of its officers. In America, as in the Netherlands, they would be able to worship as they chose. But not all of the travelers were dissidents. Some sought to better their worldly lot; among these were the military man Captain Miles Standish, the fair-haired cooper John Alden and the nubile Priscilla Mullins—all destined to be romanticized more than 200 years later by the New England poet Henry Wadsworth Longfellow in "The Courtship of Miles Standish." Moreover, the voyage, although organized by the Separatists (and approved by the Crown, which had granted the use of the land with the proviso that the settlers live peaceably), was financed by English merchants who expected the settlers to send back profitable cargoes of fish, fur and timber.

Hardheaded commercial calculations thus underlay the enterprise, and—in contrast to many previous expeditions—the participants entertained no flighty ideas of easy riches. Most of the Pilgrims were farmers and accustomed to hard work. They knew it would be difficult to set up a colony, but they were resolved to do so. With them, a new breed of Englishmen began to traverse the Atlantic.

Their voyage was the prelude to sea traffic that grew from a halting

SECOTAN

Dasamonquepuc

Roanoac

Hatorasck

Pasquenoke

WEAPEMEOC

Trinety harbor

Two ships lie off the Carolina Outer Banks as an agile pinnace threads its way to Roanoke Island in this engraving of the arrival of an English expedition in 1584. The approach inshore, wrote a later settler, was "shallowe and full of dangerous flatts"—hazards shown above by stylized wrecks along the coastal islets.

flow to a freshet to a flood. For the next two and a half centuries, sailing ships would serve as the Conestoga wagons of the Atlantic, transporting the greatest folk migration in history; before the close of the 19th Century, some 11 million human beings would make the crossing from the British Isles in the wake of the Pilgrims. The ships would also bring supplies that the settlers could not manufacture themselves—woolens to keep warm in, kettles to cook meals in, axes to fell forests with. The same ships would carry back a cornucopia of New World commodities—not only the fish, timber and fur that had been foreseen from the start, and the newly popular tobacco, but later such agricultural products as grain and cotton. With that exchange of goods—manufactures westbound, resources eastbound—the 3,000-mile reach between the Old World and North America was to become the arena of the busiest, most disputed commerce in all the seven seas.

A turning point in the efforts to colonize North America had occurred about a decade and a half before the Pilgrims embarked. In April of 1607, three English vessels—the 100-ton *Susan Constant,* the 40-ton *God-*

speed and the 20-ton *Discovery*—poked into the James River in Virginia and landed 105 settlers at a site they named Jamestown. Their venture had already suffered serious setbacks: Thirty-nine passengers had perished at sea, probably from scurvy and dysentery. The survivors seemed no more likely to thrive on land: Many were gentlemen who had sailed to the New World to find gold, not to engage in such distasteful work as farming.

Luckily for these misguided argonauts, the expedition included a remarkable man named John Smith, who would not only prove the savior of Jamestown but would also do more than any other single individual to set the great transatlantic migration in motion.

Although he was only 27 years old, Smith was already worldly-wise. A soldier of fortune, he had traveled across much of Europe, venturing as far afield as the steppes of Russia. On one journey he passed through Mainz, Germany, where Johann Gutenberg had established the first printing press almost two centuries before. Smith was a worthy heir to that legacy; he would be an uncommonly prolific writer of tracts in years to come.

In Virginia, Smith demonstrated superb organizational talents. He cheered the colonists when they were discouraged and diseased, conciliated rival factions, and persuaded what he called the "distracted

The 40-ton Godspeed, the 100-ton Susan Constant and the 20-ton Discovery maneuver for anchorage off the Virginia coast in 1607, prior to landing the founders of Jamestown, England's first permanent settlement in America. Seventeenth Century passenger ships generally crossed the Atlantic in convoy, so that if one was disabled by storm or fire, another might come to her rescue.

lubberly gluttons" to give up their quest for nonexistent gold and instead perform the manual labor that would keep them alive. He saw to it that the colony's first well was dug, began the manufacture of soap, had nets and traps made for fishing, and directed the planting of potatoes and melon seeds brought from England. On top of that, he assembled cargoes of timber and shipped them back to England. Those cargoes gave the English backers of the expedition a return on their investment, and simultaneously enabled the Jamestown colonists to purchase the supplies they needed from home.

In the fall of 1609, while traveling down the James River, John Smith suffered a freak accident. Precisely what happened is unclear, but evidently a spark from a musket or from a tobacco pipe ignited a powder bag that Smith was holding on his lap. He jumped overboard to douse the fire, and when his companions pulled him back on board he had a serious burn. Unable to lead the settlers in their search for food for the coming winter, he sailed for home. But he had given Jamestown the will to survive, and—alone among the early colonizing efforts north of Spanish-held Florida—it did.

Smith was back in the New World in 1614, this time involved in a wholly different enterprise: A pair of London merchants had sent him out with two ships to hunt whales. Reaching Monhegan Island off present-day Maine and finding no whales, he pragmatically filled the ships with codfish. But the trip was to yield a far larger bounty. Before returning with the fish, Smith sailed down the coast as far south as Cape Cod, mapping it bay by bay, inlet by inlet, and bestowing such familiar English place names as Plymouth, Dartmouth and Cambridge on sites that struck his fancy. On returning to England in 1616, Smith turned his findings into a volume entitled *A Description of New England*, thus giving a new name to the boundless territory previously known as Northern Virginia. Thereafter, he would be indefatigable in promoting the colonization of America.

Smith envisioned more clearly than any of his predecessors the enormous possibilities of the New World. In America there was "no want of anything but industrious people," he wrote. Emigrating to a near-empty continent, a highly motivated laborer could achieve a livelihood unlike any to be hoped for in the Old World, Smith argued. The right people traveling westward would produce the right goods to freight eastward in an endless circle of migration and trade. If a person "have but the taste of virtue and magnanimity, what to such a mind can be more pleasant than planting and building a foundation for his posterity?" he asked. He wrote of this new land that its earth was fertile and its water pure, and asserted that "of all the four parts of the world that I have yet seen not inhabited, could I have but means to transport a colony, I would rather live here than anywhere."

Smith was eager to get back to America; in fact, he wanted to sail on the *Mayflower* as guide and adviser to her passengers and crew. But the Pilgrims turned him down—preferring, Smith complained, "to save charges" because "my books and maps were much better cheap to teach them, than myself." The accusation may have been justified: His books and maps were indeed carried aboard the *Mayflower*. John Smith had to

Apprenticeship in adventure

When Captain John Smith sailed for Virginia at the age of 26, he was already well acquainted with the dangers—and opportunities—to be found in alien lands. The son of a tenant farmer, Smith first left England when he was about 16, hoping to see the world and find some challenge as a soldier. If his autobiography is to be believed—and there is no reason to doubt its broad outlines, at least—his ambition was soon realized.

Smith began by joining the Dutch rebels in their fight against the Spaniards in the Netherlands. After rounding out his martial education by reading Machiavelli's *The Art of War* and learning to joust, he decided to "trie his fortune against the Turkes" in a war between the Holy Roman and Ottoman Empires then raging in Hungary and Transylvania. He sailed toward the fray on a ship filled with French Catholic pilgrims. Apparently taking the brawny foreigner for a heretical pirate, they pitched him overboard. Smith swam to an island and resumed his journey on another ship.

In Hungary, Smith distinguished himself at an obscure battle. Before the fight, Smith had taught one of the officers how to send messages at night with torches; when the Turks attacked and divided the forces, Smith used torches to signal the officer and coordinate a counterattack. The Turks were routed and Smith earned the rank of captain.

Later his battalion moved on to a Turkish-held city he called Regall and began a protracted siege. During a lull, the Turks challenged the Christians to single combat on horseback—and Smith, naturally, picked up the gauntlet. He dispatched one opponent by running his lance through the Turk's visor. A second withstood Smith's lance but was wounded by his pistol. A third opponent survived the pistol, then dealt the captain such a staggering blow that he lost his battle-ax. Just as the Turk was closing in for another swipe, Smith drew out his broadsword and—exhibiting dexterity "beyond all mens expectation," he reported—managed to stab the Turk in the back.

But even Smith was no match for the horde of saber-wielding warriors—near 40,000, he estimated—who bore down on his battalion at a mountain pass south of Transylvania in 1602. He was captured and sold into slavery—a fate he escaped by killing his master with a threshing bat.

The young adventurer returned to England in 1604, stopping en route to collect a letter from the Prince of Transylvania granting him a coat of arms for valor. But Smith was not one to rest on his laurels. He was soon off to the New World to risk life and limb again in search of lasting fame.

The daring deeds of Captain John Smith are summarized in a multiepisode engraving from his autobiography. The illustrations are arranged in chronological order—except for the first two in the bottom row, which are unaccountably reversed.

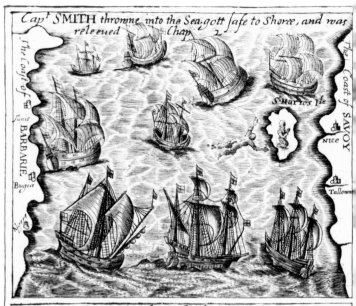

13

Part of the Trauels of Capt IOHN SMITH amongst TVRKES, TARTARS and others, extracted out of the HISTORY by IOHN PAYN

How hee releeued OLVMPAGH by a stratagem of Lights Chap. 4

The Siege of REGALL in Transiluania Chap. 7

His Combat with GRVALGO Capt of threehundred horsmen Chap. 7.

How he slew BONNY:MVLGRO Chap. 7

Three TVRKS heads in a banner giuen him for Armes Chap. 8

P. Sigismundus
pro Christo et patria
P. Moyses
MRten Dr sculptor
How he was presented to Prince SIGISMVNDVS. Chap. 8.

Capt SMITH Killeth the BASHAW of Nalbrits and on his horse escapeth. Chap. 7.

London Printed by Iames Reeue

console himself with the sour-grapes reflection that the departing Pilgrims would be "pestered" in their "leaking unwholesome ship, lying wet" for the duration of the voyage.

The Pilgrims had planned to cross in midsummer, as soon as the *Speedwell* and the *Mayflower* joined each other in Southampton, but a series of problems threw their schedule into disarray. First they were delayed by haggling over the terms of the contract with their merchant sponsors. The contract was to run for seven years, after which the profits were to be divided between the sponsoring merchants and the colonists. The colonists wanted two clauses added to the agreement. One was that they be allowed to work two days a week for themselves, instead of for the company. The other was that their houses, gardens and lots be excluded from the profits to be divided at the end of the seven years. The merchants held that the houses, gardens and lots should be common property; the colonists protested that they would work more diligently—"with borrowed houres from their sleep"—if they knew they would own their homes in the end. When the two camps reached an impasse, the colonists refused to sign the document, and on August 5, 1620, they set sail without a contract. The matter would never be resolved.

Shortly after they were under way, the *Speedwell* developed leaks, and both ships put back from the English Channel to Dartmouth so she could be repaired. After almost two weeks, they made a new start, but the *Speedwell* continued to leak badly, and the expedition turned around once again and sailed into Plymouth for more repairs. There the Pilgrims concluded that the *Speedwell* was simply unseaworthy and ought to be given up. Her provisions were transferred to the *Mayflower*. Fourteen passengers and 20 crewmen decided they had had enough of this fitful undertaking and headed for home.

On September 16, with the autumn gale season upon them, the remaining Pilgrims made yet another start. The *Mayflower* carried 101 passengers, 31 of them children, plus two pet dogs and a crew of 34. The ship's captain was Christopher Jones, a quarter owner of the *Mayflower* and an experienced seaman; he had sailed for years in the Mediterranean wine trade and more recently had carried cloth and hides to the ports of Bordeaux and La Rochelle.

The *Mayflower* herself was a reassuringly proportioned ship—90 feet in length and 25 feet in the beam. Vessels categorized as "ships" then ranged in size from 40 to 400 tons. At 180 tons, the *Mayflower* was larger than all three of the first Jamestown ships put together.

As a three-masted square-rigger, she also represented the latest in sailing-ship design. Her mainmast, judging by contemporary shipping records, was 80 feet high, her foremast 58 feet, her mizzenmast 42 feet. Her bowsprit extended 57 feet forward from the bow of the ship. All these spars tapered from a sturdy two feet at their base to a mere eight inches at the top.

She carried a full wardrobe of sails, in three different weights for different winds. They were made of heavy flax canvas, hand-woven so fine that it was said to be as strong as chain armor. Along the sails' edges were slotted holes bound in leather to prevent fraying by the ropes that

Simon Paßæus sculpsit.
Robert Clerke Excudit.

Bearing a likeness of its maker, John Smith, this remarkably accurate chart of the New England coast guided the Mayflower and many other 17th Century ships to safe landfalls. As he ranged along the shore in 1614, Smith gave promising sites such English town names as Plymouth and Boston—labels later adopted by early settlers, but often applied to places far from their chart locations.

controlled them and held them to the yards. The rigging consisted of more than 400 ropes weighing eight tons in all. In the hold was another vessel, a disassembled 30-foot shallop that could be used for exploration; on one occasion, it would carry 32 men, and on another, 18 men with supplies enough to last for several days.

By all accounts the *Mayflower* was a sturdy ship, but hardly a comfortable one. With her complicated rigging and high superstructures known as castles at the bow and stern, she was top-heavy and would bob on the ocean like a cork. Captain Jones was the best off; he was housed in quarters at the stern, which he shared with his two mates. The crewmen slept in the cramped forecastle. In fair weather, the passengers had the run of the main deck, which probably measured 75 by 20 feet, but at night and in rough weather they huddled below in the dank,

A curious crowd assembles to gawk at the Pilgrim ships
Mayflower (center) and Speedwell (left) during an unscheduled
stop at the Channel port of Dartmouth on August 14, 1620.
The smaller Speedwell, which the Pilgrims intended to use as
a fishing vessel after their Atlantic crossing, leaked so
badly that even the extensive calking done at Dartmouth could
not make her right. She was subsequently abandoned at
Plymouth, and the overcrowded Mayflower continued on alone.

miasmic hold (night air was considered unhealthy—"rheumy"—in any weather). The hold was about 25 feet long and 15 feet across, with a ceiling so low a man could not stand upright. The space was cluttered with the passengers' possessions—bundles of clothing, cooking implements, guns and tools, plus some 20,000 pounds of dried biscuit (known to seamen as hard tack) and 30 bushels of oatmeal to get the Pilgrims through the voyage and a winter at their destination in the wilderness. Other vital supplies included a quantity of barley, wheat and peas for eventual planting.

In this dim, belowdecks area, there was almost no ventilation, and the only sanitary facilities available were buckets. The odor may not at first have been so offensive as on some ships, since the lingering scent of a wine cargo made for what was known as a "sweet ship." But hides and furs left a rank smell. So did the fetid bilge water, which would have been accumulating since the *Mayflower*'s first days afloat, 14 years before. Add to those the odors of the vomit of seasick passengers, of excrement, of unwashed bodies, of maggoty food, and the stench would have been sour indeed.

During fair weather the *Mayflower*'s passengers were able to cook in turns over small braziers set on deck in boxes of sand to catch the sparks. There was no cooking when the seas were rough, and at such times the passengers subsisted on biscuit, salted meat, dried fish, cheese, dried beans and peas, washed down with beer. Bradford's journal does not say so, but within a few weeks most of the passengers would have been too ill to eat, having succumbed to the fevers and dysentery that almost always broke out on cramped sailing ships.

Those who could make it up on deck found diversion in watching the crew perform the endless routines of ship maintenance. One critical task was calking—tamping fibrous wadding into any leaky seams of the hull. The ship's hempen rigging always needed readjustment, since the ropes shrank when wet and stretched when dry. In addition, the bilge required constant pumping out, and the deck had to be scraped and cleaned every day.

The passengers' fascination with the workings of this little seagoing world was spiced with a sense of lurking danger. They were taking the perilous northern route to America—the course used by fishermen heading for the Grand Banks. Here, in an expanse of ocean lacking islands where mariners might find shelter, prevailing winds called westerlies blow steadily against the bows of outbound vessels and regularly give rise to fierce Arctic gales. European mariners had circled the globe, and they knew of no other lengthy stretch of ocean where the weather was so consistently tempestuous. The *Mayflower* would head north toward Greenland to avoid the opposing flow of the Gulf Stream, then turn west, tacking into the wind, and move with the Arctic current toward Newfoundland before steering south to the New England coast.

The westerlies are part of a pattern of strong winds and currents perpetually circling the floating algae of the Sargasso Sea. An alternative route to America—pioneered by Christopher Columbus and used by the Jamestown settlers—exploited a more benign part of this pattern: the trade winds that blow from east to west. Ships taking the southern course headed down past the Bay of Biscay, continuing on to reprovision in the Azores or the Canaries before turning toward America. They would put in again in the West Indies. Because of the islands, there was much less distance between landfalls, but the entire trip consumed at least three months, and sometimes five, as opposed to an average of eight to 10 weeks on the northern route, and the Pilgrims had concluded that the swifter crossing was the safer one.

Knowing that some bad weather during the crossing was inevitable, one Pilgrim had predicted to a friend that they would all soon be "meat for ye fishes." Such a fate very nearly did befall John Howland, the 27-year-old secretary to the company's governor, John Carver. Seeking relief from the fetid atmosphere of the hold one stormy day, Howland went on deck and was promptly swept overboard by a wave. He managed to grab a topsail halyard, however, and was pulled back on board with a boat hook. He would live to the age of 80 and, as Bradford recalled, "became a profitable member both in church and commonwealth." Still, his experience underlined for the other passengers just how quickly the sea could claim a victim.

The passengers soon learned from the crewmen to spot foul weather in the making. The telltale signs might be extremely low-lying clouds, a ring around the moon, the sight of a scurrying school of dolphin or, with only a light breeze, a strange, heaving swell to the ocean. As a storm approached, the air would grow heavy, and lightning would flash in the distance. With furious activity, the crew would begin to furl the sails, starting with the fore-, main- and mizzen-topsails. And then the heavy winds would hit, howling through the rigging and causing the vessel to thrash so violently that the crewmen could hardly hold on to the long whipstaff that controlled the rudder. In some instances the ship tossed aimlessly in the waves for days at a time before the winds subsided—even though, according to Bradford's diary, every last sail was furled and the ship rode under bare poles.

Repeated battering of this sort strained the hull to the breaking point. In the middle of a particularly savage gale, the Pilgrims noticed that "one of the main beams in the midships was bowed and cracked," as Bradford remembered. The discovery caused near panic among the passengers, and even the sea-wise Captain Jones considered the matter serious enough to call his officers together to consider returning to England. "In examining all opinions, the master and others affirmed they knew the ship to be strong and firm under water," Bradford recalled. To remedy the immediate problem, they produced an implement that Bradford described as "a great iron screw" (its exact nature remains unknown), and used it to push the cracked beam back into place. They then reinforced the beam with a timber wedged against the lower deck, and the *Mayflower* sailed on.

In addition to the stresses imposed on the ship, every storm increased the uncertainty as to the voyagers' whereabouts. In the 17th Century, navigation on the high seas was primitive. A captain groped across the ocean with little more than a compass and a backstaff, a device that measured the altitude of the sun to yield a rough estimate of the ship's latitude. He had no device for determining longitude, and to determine his east-west progress he had to rely on dead reckoning—a calculation based on the vessel's speed through the water and an estimate of the effect of any current.

Speed was measured with the aid of a log line, a rope attached to a piece of wood, with knots set 48 feet apart. As the line was paid out over the stern, a large sandglass, suspended from a hook so as to remain more or less perpendicular when the ship pitched and rolled, measured off a set period of time. From the number of knots that ran out during that period, Captain Jones or First Mate John Clark could estimate how fast the ship was traveling. Estimates of the effects of currents were based simply on passages made by earlier vessels, there being no direct way for those on board to measure the current's velocity. The truth is that, soon after leaving land behind, Jones and Clark could have had only the vaguest notion of their location.

As the days wore on, uncertainty and fear mounted, and tempers inevitably grew short. One crewman in particular took to harrying the passengers, cursing and jeering at them when they fell sick. He told them, Bradford said, "that he hoped to help to cast half of them overboard before they came to their journey's end." But before the first half of the trip was over, "it pleased God to smite this young man with a grievous disease, of which he died in a desperate manner, and so it was he himself the first that was thrown overboard." The man's death "was an astonishment to all his fellows for they noted it to be the just hand of God upon him," Bradford went on. Although Bradford does not mention it, the passengers were probably accorded better treatment by the crew thereafter, since seamen were notoriously superstitious.

This was the only death among the crew on the crossing, and only a single passenger perished; he was a young servant, William Butten, who succumbed to an unnamed disease as the ship neared the American coast. At about the same time, a baby was born to a couple named Elizabeth and Stephen Hopkins. They christened him Oceanus, and he grew up to be a sailor.

In early November, birds were seen in the sky and the passengers smelled what in many 17th Century sea diaries was called the "sweet perfume" of the American forests; it emanated from the pine, spruce and balsam that grew to the shoreline. On November 9, the lookout in the crow's-nest sighted land—high, sandy bluffs along the outer shore of Cape Cod, near the present-day town of Truro. The ship did not put in. "After some deliberation," Bradford recorded, the travelers "resolved to stand for the southward to find someplace about Hudson's River for their habitation." The *Mayflower* moved down the coast until, as Bradford related, she "fell in amongst dangerous shoals and roaring breakers." At this point, the leaders of the company decided to go back to the coastline they had already seen; at least they knew it could be approached. So, keeping well out to sea, the captain sailed northward, then slowly rounded the tip of the Cape and entered Cape Cod Bay.

On the 11th of November, after 65 days at sea, the *Mayflower* dropped anchor off today's Provincetown, one of the most protected harbors on the entire seaboard. For the Pilgrims, it was an emotional moment. Brad-

With a work party on board, a shallop leaves the ice-encrusted Mayflower and heads toward the Plymouth shore. Throughout the bitter winter of 1620-1621, the Pilgrims used the Mayflower for shelter while they pegged out plots and felled trees for permanent dwellings.

ford recorded that they "fell upon their knees and blessed the God of Heaven" for delivering them "from all the perils and miseries" of the ocean, permitting them "again to set their feet on the firm and stable earth, their proper element."

Proper, perhaps, but bleak as well. "They had now no friends to welcome them nor inns to entertain them or refresh their weatherbeaten bodies," Bradford pointed out; "not houses or much less towns to repair to, to seek for succour." A cold wind was blowing, and soon it brought snow. Although they had to remain with the ship, they made several excursions ashore, wading through the near-freezing water—women to do washing, men to reconnoiter the countryside (they quickly discovered there were Indians about), and the ship's carpenter and his helpers to begin reassembling the shallop, which had been badly battered from knocking about in the hold during the crossing.

More than two weeks were spent in patching the shallop and stepping its single mast. That done, Miles Standish set off with a group of men to investigate the coast. Two days later he returned with the judgment that the Cape, with its tangled thickets of wind-stunted trees, was a poor place to settle. On December 6, Standish and his advance party were back in the shallop, coasting farther down the inner shore of the Cape to what is now called Wellfleet Bay. There, the men waded through shallow water to the beach, marched inland and discovered an Indian encampment, some baskets of corn, and the remains of a beached whale that the Indians had carved up for a meal. The colonists settled down and spent a quiet night, presumably after helping themselves to the food. The next day, however, the Indians appeared and immediately loosed a volley of arrows at the trespassers. They were driven off by musket fire. Although no one was hurt in the brief exchange, the Cape seemed more than ever an unfriendly spot.

The scouting party now headed for the mainland across Cape Cod Bay, weathering a storm that knocked the shallop's mast overboard. They came upon a more promising place of refuge, with fresh-water brooks flowing down to the shore and land that had once been planted in corn. Elated, Standish and his group sailed back across the bay, informed the rest of the passengers of the discovery and proposed that the *Mayflower* follow the shallop there. She did, and on December 15—more than three months after leaving England, and nearly five months after the vanguard of Pilgrims had departed from Holland on the *Speedwell*— the *Mayflower* dropped anchor at the small harbor marked on John Smith's map as Plymouth.

Whatever hopes had been raised by landing were quick to dissipate. The weather was mild as New England winters go, but until the Pilgrims could build shelter ashore they had to live on the ship. Before long they were stricken with what Bradford called "the general visitation"—probably a combination of scurvy, pneumonia and a virulent, fast-acting form of tuberculosis, and most likely brought on because the travelers were weakened from the rigors and the poor diet of the crossing. Four passengers had already died while the *Mayflower* lay at Provincetown; now others succumbed one after another. By the time the disease had run its course, only 53—scarcely half the original Pilgrims and half the crew—remained alive. The victims included John Carver, who was succeeded as governor by Bradford. At the lowest point, only half a dozen of the band remained well, and they constantly hazarded their own health by caring for the sick, cooking meals, changing bedding and performing other functions that, as Bradford delicately put it, "quesie stomacks cannot endure to hear named."

As health returned, the survivors turned their attention landward. They hacked away at the forest, raising a few one-room thatched cottages from sticks and mud plaster. From a friendly Indian named Squanto, who picked up some English, they learned to catch eels and small fish in the streams. They shot wild turkeys and deer, and gathered oysters, clams and lobsters along the shore. That simple fare got them through the winter. On March 21, the last of the surviving passengers removed themselves and their baggage from the anchored *Mayflower*.

The Pilgrims' understanding with the merchants who financed the expedition had called for the ship to return to England with such cargo as might be raised "by trade, traffic, trucking, working, fishing or any other means of any person or persons" in the company. But they had been forced to work so hard just to stay alive that assembling a cargo had been out of the question. Captain Jones, having his own interest in the commercial life of the ship, determined to go back to England, empty hold or no, and on April 5 he was ready to set sail. He offered passage to anyone who wished to return. Not a single Pilgrim accepted.

Instead, they settled into their frail village and carved out a new life for themselves. As spring wore on and softened the ground, they planted

Wanderings of a legendary rock

Mid-19th Century tourists peer at Plymouth Rock through a fence—protection from souvenir hunters' chisels.

When French political observer Alexis de Tocqueville visited America in the 1830s, he was struck by the veneration that Americans paid to Plymouth Rock as the site of the Pilgrims' landing in the New World. "Here is a stone which the feet of a few poor fugitives pressed for an instant," he wrote, "and this stone becomes famous."

Indeed, the Pilgrim feet may not have pressed that particular stone at all. More concerned with survival than with documenting their historic firsts, the Pilgrims failed to record exactly where they came ashore in 1620. But in 1741, when Plymouth shipowners undertook to build a wharf for the vessels calling at the port, Thomas Faunce, a 95-year-old church elder, stepped forward in dismay. Pilgrims known to him in his youth, he claimed, had reported debarking on a certain granite boulder in the harbor—and the proposed wharf would obscure this natural monument. In the presence of a delegation of citizens, Faunce kissed the rock and, by one account, tearfully "bid to it an everlasting adieu." The dramatic gesture spared the rock and spawned a legend.

By the time Tocqueville wrote about it nearly a century later, the rock—or, more accurately, a fragment of it weighing several tons—stood in a place of honor in the town square, having been hauled there by 30 yoke of oxen in 1774, on the eve of the Revolution. But its peregrinations were not over. In 1880 the fragment was carried back to the shore and reunited with its massive base under a stone canopy of elaborate Victorian arches. Later, the canopy and the old wharves were removed, and the area was landscaped so that, at high tide, the surf would pound Plymouth Rock just as it had when the Pilgrims arrived.

the barley, wheat and peas that they had brought from England, and—with Squanto's help—they laid out 20 acres of corn. The following autumn they harvested their first crop (Squanto's native corn did better than the imported barley, wheat and peas). The village at Plymouth now had a number of small houses, and a common hall was going up. In an expansive feeling of well-being, the colonists staged a three-day feast of thanksgiving, inviting Squanto and some of his fellow tribesmen, whom they had befriended.

On November 11, 1621—a year to the day after the Pilgrims had first touched land—a 55-ton ship called the *Fortune* sailed in and dropped anchor in the harbor. She carried with her 35 more settlers—"without so much as bisket-cake or any other victialls," Bradford noted ruefully—and she also brought a harsh letter from the *Mayflower's* leading backer. "That you sent no lading in the ship is wonderful, and worthily distasted," he wrote, demanding that the Pilgrims "give us account as particularly as you can, how our moneys were laid out." Bradford responded with a brief summation of the difficulties the Pilgrims had sustained, pointing out that the loss of "industrious men's lives cannot be valued at any price." And the Pilgrims now made amends, loading the *Fortune* with beaver and otter skins and clapboards that they had sawed out of the bountiful timber. The *Fortune* returned to England in late December—but minus her cargo, which had been seized by a French warship off the coast of France. The first round of the commercial bonanza envisioned by John Smith was off to a sorry start.

The next wave of arrivals consisted of another group of religious dissenters, the Puritans, who voyaged to the New World during the 1630s in a sudden rush that came to be known as the Great Migration. More intolerant than the Separatists who preceded them, the Puritans were driven by a compulsion to rid both the church and the state of pomp and circumstance—and a determination to vest in the people decisions pertaining to both. Under the leadership of a stern governor, John Winthrop—a member of the landed gentry who envisioned New England as the site of great estates worked by hired labor—the Puritans had begun assembling a fleet of 17 ships at Southampton in the winter of 1629-1630. On March 29 the first seven ships departed, with some 700 passengers. The other vessels followed one by one.

For all, the crossing was troubled and stormy. So much freight and livestock had been loaded on some vessels that horses and cattle had to be thrown overboard at sea to prevent the ships from capsizing. Governor Winthrop wrote of passengers "who lay groaning" with sickness on his flagship, the *Arbella*. He did not indicate how many of the company failed to survive.

The *Arbella* reached Massachusetts Bay on June 10, and all the other vessels made landfall in succeeding weeks. As soon as the Puritans had settled in this new land, they sent word for their fellow dissidents in England to follow. By the end of the decade, some 16,000 Puritans had reached America, and they rimmed the 75-mile-long coast of Massachusetts Bay with little villages.

The newcomers had an easier entry than their predecessors; on arrival, they found fresh food, corn, cattle and lumber available to them. And they brought with them an abundance of plows, guns and other hardware for which the older settlers were only too eager to barter the fruits of their labor.

In the 1640s, emigration from England slowed dramatically. Under the stirring rhetoric and efficient military organization of a firebrand named Oliver Cromwell, rebels in England sought to seize power for the very reasons that the Puritans had left their country. When Cromwell succeeded in driving King Charles I into exile, Puritans no longer needed to seek a haven across the Atlantic. Meanwhile, even fishing vessels ceased to make the crossing for cod; as civil war raged, Royalists pressed into naval service any vessel they could find on the high seas.

In the colonies themselves, material well-being declined as immigration did; plows and guns wore out, and hardly anyone was bringing in replacements. "All foreign commodities grew scarce and our own of no price," Winthrop wrote. But the isolation had another effect that would in the long run prove beneficial. "These straits," he wrote, "set our people to work to provide fish, clapboards, plank, etc., and to look out to the West Indies for a trade."

The colonists helped themselves to the plentiful cod, haddock, pollack, hake and mackerel they found in New England waters, and prepared export cargoes of dried fish and cod oil. The towns of Salem, Gloucester, Marblehead and others up and down the coast were transformed into important fishing centers. In the single year of 1641, more than 300,000 codfish were hauled into Massachusetts ports and readied for shipment across the Atlantic.

To make their transport possible, Governor Winthrop—who had long since found that the region was too barren for the plantations he had envisioned—launched Massachusetts on the serious business of shipbuilding. Some shipbuilding had been done since the earliest days of settlement, but at first it was for purposes of coastal exploration or to replace vessels that had been wrecked or simply to return home. For example, escape was the motive of a group of Englishmen who had settled Stage Island in the mouth of the Kennebec River in Maine during the early years of the century; discouraged by the climate, they built a 30-ton, single-masted pinnace, the *Virginia*, and in the spring of 1608 sailed her back to the mother country (so sturdy was the little vessel that she was used on several other transatlantic expeditions).

A number of shipwrights, ship's carpenters and sawyers had been among the Puritans who came in the years of the Great Migration, and they soon put their skills to work. In 1631 a 30-ton bark called the *Blessing of the Bay* was launched on the Mystic River at the Puritan settlement of Medford. She was used to carry timber and fish to other ports along the seaboard. In 1636 Medford saw the launching of by far the largest colonial ship built to date, the 120-ton *Desire*, which entered the transatlantic trade.

But much greater things lay ahead; Winthrop aimed at nothing less than creating an industry. He exempted shipbuilders from service in the militia and, to lure additional workmen into the business, he established water-driven sawmills—a new technological development that English

The 30-ton pinnace Virginia—the first
vessel built by English settlers in
the American colonies—cruises the New
England coast in this 20th Century
watercolor. Constructed in 1607 at a short-
lived settlement at the mouth of the
Kennebec River in Maine, she carried the
discouraged colonists home—then
returned repeatedly to America before
being wrecked on the Irish coast.

shipyards had not yet adopted. Under the spur of his encouragement, the port of Salem in 1641 constructed a 300-tonner, the Mary Ann. In 1642, Boston launched the 160-ton Trial—and launched itself as a shipbuilding center to reckon with; between 1643 and 1646 Boston turned out five new ships that ranged in size from 200 tons to 400 tons. Soon these ships were plying the northern route across the Atlantic—and voyaging south to the West Indies as well. Simultaneously, Boston developed facilities to repair and outfit foreign ships that called there.

The ships that came down the colonial ways in these years were for the most part financed by English merchants—and with good reason: Ships could be built faster and more cheaply in the colonies than in the homeland. But even with long-distance ownership, the newly aggressive shipbuilding business had immediate effects on colonial well-being. The rising demand for timber made logging camps proliferate—not only in Massachusetts, but in neighboring Maine and New Hampshire as well—and out of such camps would come many a permanent village. The increase in ships invited the growth of companion businesses to produce sailcloth, cordage and ship's fittings. Meanwhile, flour mills sprang up, providing another commodity to trade in the West Indies for sugar and molasses. And traffic in molasses encouraged a new colonial industry: the distillation of rum.

One way or another, virtually all the colonists, whatever their primary callings, benefited from this burgeoning life of the sea. In fall and winter, when their fields were at rest, farmers went offshore to fish; and during the long evenings, any man who lived near the woods and was handy with a knife might whittle barrel staves for the casks that seagoing cargoes traveled in. Moreover, as New Englanders prospered through their maritime connections, they began enlarging their horizons. The first step of ambitious colonists was to buy into partnership with shipowning London merchants, and earn a percentage of the profits on imports and exports. The next step, inevitably, was to commission ships of their own and keep all of the profits.

During the 18 years of civil strife in the mother country, New England merchants continued to expand their maritime dealings, and by 1660, when the King was restored to the throne, they had their own fishing fleets and a comfortable grip on trade with southern Europe and the West Indies. A decade and a half later, although the majority of ships built in the colonies were still English-owned, Massachusetts merchants held title to 430 vessels that ranged in size from 30 to 250 tons. Shipbuilding, moreover, had spread to other settlements throughout the northern and middle Atlantic colonies.

Meanwhile, other settlements were beginning in the South—but on a different pattern. Instead of building towns, Virginians wound up developing plantations of ever larger size. Nature had blessed the South with richer soil than New England's. This soil, along with the climate, proved ideal for a mild and sweet strain of tobacco that originated in South America and was first brought to Jamestown from England in 1612 by a settler named John Rolfe. In 1616, just four years after Rolfe's first planting, 2,300 pounds of what became known as Virginia leaf were shipped to England. The next year, 10 tons of tobacco were sent to the mother country. Before the century ended, hundreds of ships would be needed to transport a single year's tobacco crop of 11,000 tons.

Wherever and however they lived, all those who came to America had something more than an economic connection with the sea. The Atlantic crossing was part of everyone's background, a part of the American consciousness. A Puritan named Francis Higginson wrote of how "the sea roared and the waves tossed us horridly" and how "it was fearful dark and the mariners made us afraid with their running here and there, and loud crying one to another to pull at this or that rope." A Virginian recalled how, in the hold coming over, nobody could "fetch his breath by reason there arises such a funk in the night that it causes putrefaction of blood and breedeth disease much like the plague." A passenger who crossed the Atlantic on the *Virginia Merchant* during the Great Migration left a spine-chilling account of what happened when the vessel ran out of food: "Women and children made dismal cries and grievous complaints. The infinite number of rats that all the voyage had been our plague, we now were glad to make our prey to feed on; and as they were ensnared and taken, a well-grown rat was sold for 16

A broadside urges colonists bound for Virginia in 1622 to outfit themselves with "Eight bushels of Meale," "Five felling Axes," "Nailes of all sorts," and numerous other items as a hedge against the "inconveniencies" of short supplies in the New World. Drawn by the promise of 50 acres of land apiece, settlers poured into Virginia at the rate of about 1,000 annually.

THE INCONVENIENCIES

THAT HAVE HAPPENED TO SOME PER-
SONS WHICH HAVE TRANSPORTED THEMSELVES

from *England* to *Virginia*, vvithout prouifions neceffary to fuftaine themfelues, hath
greatly hindred the *Progreffe* of that noble *Plantation*: For preuention of the like diforders
heereafter, that no man fuffer, either through ignorance or mifinformation; it is thought re-
quifite to publifh this fhort declaration: wherein is contained a particular of fuch necef-
faries, as either priuate families or fingle perfons fhall haue caufe to furnifh themfelues with, for their better
fupport at their firft landing in Virginia; whereby alfo greater numbers may receiue in part,
directions how to prouide themfelues.

Apparrell.	li.	s.	d.
One Monmouth Cap———	∞	01	10
Three falling bands———	—	01	03
Three fhirts———	—	07	06
One wafte-coate———	—	02	02
One fuite of Canuafe———	—	07	06
One fuite of Frize———	—	10	00
One fuite of Cloth———	—	15	00
Three paire of Irifh ftockins———	—	04	—
Foure paire of fhooes———	—	08	08
One paire of garters———	—	00	10
One doozen of points———	—	00	03
One paire of Canuafe fheets———	—	08	00
Seuen ells of Canuafe, to make a bed and boulfter, to be filled in *Virginia* 8.s.—— One Rug for a bed 8.s. which with the bed feruing for two men, halfe is———	—	08	00
Fiue ells coorfe Canuafe, to make a bed at Sea for two men, to be filled with ftraw, iiij.s.—— One coorfe Rug at Sea for two men, will coft vj.s. is for one———	—	05	00
	04	00	00

Apparrell for one man, and fo after the rate for more.

Victuall.	li.	s.	d.
Eight bufhels of Meale———	02	00	00
Two bufhels of peafe at 3.s.———	—	06	00
Two bufhels of Oatemeale 4.s.6.d.———	—	09	00
One gallon of *Aquauitæ*———	—	02	06
One gallon of Oyle———	—	03	06
Two gallons of Vineger 1.s.———	—	02	00
	03	03	00

For a whole yeere for one man, and fo for more after the rate.

Armes.	li.	s.	d.
One Armour compleat, light———	—	17	00
One long Peece, fiue foot or fiue and a halfe, neere Musket bore———	01	02	—
One fword———	—	05	—
One belt———	—	01	—
One bandaleere———	—	01	06
Twenty pound of powder———	—	18	00
Sixty pound of fhot or lead, Piftoll and Goofe fhot———	—	05	00
	03	09	06

For one man, but if halfe of your men haue armour it is fufficient fo that all haue Peeces and fwords.

Tooles.	li.	s.	d.
Fiue broad howes at 2.s. a piece———	—	10	—
Fiue narrow howes at 16.d. a piece———	—	06	08
Two broad Axes at 3.s.8.d. a piece———	—	07	04
Fiue felling Axes at 18.d. a piece———	—	07	06
Two fteele hand fawes at 16.d. a piece———	—	02	08
Two two-hand-fawes at 5.s. a piece———	—	10	—
One whip-faw, fet and filed with box, file, and wreft———	—	10	—
Two hammers 12.d. a piece———	—	02	00
Three fhouels 18.d. a piece———	—	04	06
Two fpades at 18.d. a piece———	—	03	—
Two augers 6.d. a piece———	—	01	00
Six chiffels 6.d. a piece———	—	03	00
Two percers ftocked 4.d. a piece———	—	00	08
Three gimlets 2.d. a piece———	—	00	06
Two hatchets 21.d. a piece———	—	03	06
Two froues to cleaue pale 18.d.———	—	03	00
Two hand-bills 20. a piece———	—	03	04
One grindleftone 4.s.———	—	04	00
Nailes of all forts to the value of———	02	00	—
Two Pickaxes———	—	03	—
	06	02	08

For a family of 6. perfons and fo after the rate for more.

Houfhold Implements.	li.	s.	d.
One Iron Pot———	00	07	—
One kettle———	—	06	—
One large frying-pan———	—	02	06
One gridiron———	—	01	06
Two skillets———	—	05	—
One fpit———	—	02	—
Platters, difhes, fpoones of wood———	—	04	—
	01	08	00

For a family of. 6. perfons, and fo for more or leffe after the rate.

For Suger, Spice, and fruit, and at Sea for 6. men——— ∞ | 12 | 06
So the full charge of Apparrell, Victuall, Armes, Tooles, and houfhold ftuffe, and after this rate for each perfon, will amount vnto about the fumme of——— 12 | 10 | —
The paffage of each man is——— 06 | 00 | —
The fraight of thefe prouifions for a man, will bee about halfe a Tun, which is——— 01 | 10 | —

So the whole charge will amount to about——— 20 | 00 | 00

*Nets, hookes, lines, and a tent muft be added, if the number of people be grea-
ter, as alfo fome kine.
And this is the vfuall proportion that the Virginia Company doe
beftow vpon their Tenants which they fend*

Whofoeuer tranfports himfelfe or any other at his owne charge vnto *Virginia*, fhall for each perfon fo tranfported before Midfummer 1625.
haue to him and his heires for euer fifty Acres of Land vpon a firft, and fifty Acres vpon a fecond diuifion.

Imprinted at London by Felix Kyngston. 1622.

shillings as a market rate. Nay, before the voyage did end, a woman great with child offered 20 shillings for a rat, which the proprietor refusing, the woman died."

To many, the Atlantic crossing must have been their single greatest ordeal of a lifetime, but it was also their greatest opportunity. The people who came to the colonies were rarely aristocrats, or even well-to-do, although a number of gentlemen arrived after the overthrow of Charles I, and there was a steady flow of wellborn second sons who had to make their own way because of the laws of primogeniture. Religious dissidents continued to come: The Huguenots—French Protestants—began settling the Carolinas in the 1680s; and the Quakers, after trying New England and being made unwelcome by the Puritans, settled in Pennsylvania at about the same time. A few who came were political prisoners exiled during and after Oliver Cromwell's years of power. A few were vagabonds and felons, sent abroad to empty the jails. A few more were destitute children who had been dispatched to Virginia in bondage by the City of London. But most emigrants—perhaps the majority even during the Puritan's Great Migration—came because they did not see a future in the Old World.

From the beginning of the 17th Century, English farmlands were being fenced off to raise sheep for woolen goods. In the switch from agriculture to commerce, many thousands of people were expelled from the land each year and forced to roam the English countryside in search of employment. Although the population of England was only five million at the start of the 17th Century, the country was widely believed to be overcrowded. An easy way to get rid of this supposed surplus, and create new markets at the same time, was to send people out across the Atlantic. Because they were destitute, perhaps as many as half of all the people who crossed the Atlantic in the 17th Century—women and children as well as men—came as indentured servants. Nine of the passengers aboard the *Mayflower*, including two or three children, had been under indenture.

In return for their passage, such servants agreed to work under terms set down in indenture papers, sometimes signed before they left England, sometimes provided by the men who bought the servants at auction in an American port. In exchange for a fixed period of labor that ranged from three to seven years—or, in the case of younger servants, that lasted until they reached their majority—they were clothed and fed; at the end of the indenture, a male servant would usually receive, as part of the written agreement, a plot of land.

In the North, indentured servants were used as farm workers, sometimes as laborers in small industries, and as household servants. In the South, where they arrived in greater numbers, they were set to work on the large plantations that, as the century progressed, replaced small holdings. It is estimated that in Maryland in the 1670s a tenth of all the white people working in the tobacco fields were under indenture.

A less fortunate group came without any promise of release from their labors: the black slaves rounded up by force in Africa. In 1619 a group of 20 blacks was unloaded from a Dutch ship in Jamestown—the first slaves to reach America. From that small beginning, an institution grew:

The Indian princess who cast her lot with Jamestown

Ætatis suæ 21. A 1616.

Matoaks als Rebecka daughter to the mighty Prince Powhatan Emperour of Attanoughkomouck als Virginia converted and baptized in the Christian faith, and Wife to the wor.ll M.r Tho: Rolff.

Pocahontas is decked out in the finery of an English lady in this portrait, which was probably copied from an engraving made during her visit to London. Her husband John is erroneously identified as Thomas.

In a chronicle of Jamestown published in 1624, Captain John Smith told of being dramatically rescued by an Indian princess 16 years earlier. According to the account, Smith was taken captive while on an exploratory mission, and was led before Chief Powhatan of the tribe that bore his name. The Indians went into a long consultation—presumably to decide their prisoner's fate—and then, to Smith's horror, forced him to the ground and prepared to "beate out his braines." But just as the warriors raised their clubs, the chief's daughter, Pocahontas, rushed forward and threw her body over his, persuading her father to spare the white man's life.

The tale was never corroborated, and historians have debated its truth ever since. But it is certain that a friendship developed between the Indian maiden and the brash, bearded Englishman—a friendship that would entangle Pocahontas in the affairs of Jamestown and shape her fate.

Beginning in 1608, Pocahontas visited the colony regularly, bringing wild game and bread to Smith and the other settlers, who "els for all this had starved with hunger," as one of them wrote. After Smith sailed for England in 1609, the colonists saw no more of Pocahontas until 1613, when they learned she was visiting the Potomac Indians, who were friendly to the settlers. By then, Powhatan's hostility had flared up again: He refused to trade with the settlers and had taken some English prisoners. In desperation, the colonists kidnapped Pocahontas and held her hostage for corn, the captives and some stolen weapons.

Powhatan was slow to respond to the colonists' demands, causing the disillusioned Pocahontas to ask whether her father valued her "lesse than old Swords, Peeces, or Axes." And before long, she decided to live permanently with her captors.

In Jamestown, Pocahontas learned English, converted to Christianity and took the name Rebecca. In time, John Rolfe—a tobacco farmer who had a hand in her education—fell in love with her and asked the colony's deputy governor for permission to marry her. The official agreed, seeing the match as a way to strengthen peace with Powhatan. The chief sent emissaries to the wedding, and harmony was restored.

In the spring of 1616, Pocahontas, her husband and infant son sailed to England at the invitation of Jamestown's investors, who hoped the exotic Indian woman would attract attention and backing for their New World ventures. To their delight, Pocahontas created a sensation. She was presented to the King and Queen and introduced to stockholders, who were all impressed that she "did not only accustome her selfe to civilitie, but still carried her selfe as the Daughter of a King," according to one account.

Oddly, though Smith was in England at the time, he did not visit Pocahontas until autumn. When he appeared, unannounced, at her door, Pocahontas was so taken aback that she had to excuse herself to regain her composure. When she returned, she explained to Smith she had thought him dead. Since he plainly was not, she reproached him for neglecting her.

Shortly after this strained and unsettling encounter, Smith left London, never to see Pocahontas again. In 1617, she fell ill—prey, perhaps, to one of the white man's diseases for which she had no immunity. She set off for home, but died before reaching the open sea. With her death, the Indians' policy of peace toward Jamestown began to crumble. In 1622, an Indian massacre claimed the lives of more than 300 colonists. Pocahontas' husband, who is known to have died that year, may have been one of the victims.

By 1670, Virginia had some 2,000 slaves, and they were looked upon as essential to the plantation system.

Slaves excepted, the patterns of life and commerce in 17th Century America had been established by the time that Massachusetts Bay asserted itself as a maritime force in the 1640s. There would be no startling new developments before the century came to a close—just steady growth. From Massachusetts, colonists fanned out to Rhode Island, New Hampshire, Maine and Connecticut. In the South, planters seeking more land moved into Maryland and the Carolinas. From the Hudson Valley, where in 1609 the Dutch had planted the colony of New Netherland (which would be annexed by England as a prize of war in 1664), settlers moved into parts of what would become New York, New Jersey and Delaware. Pennsylvania, claimed by William Penn for the Quakers, became a prosperous addition to the collection of colonies.

Year by year, more settlers, freemen and indentured servants entered each of these regions. The colonies slowly grew—to some 160,000 people in 1660 and 190,000 in 1685. Despite periodic arrivals of groups of Swedes in Delaware, Dutch in New York, French in the Carolinas, and a few Germans and Poles in New England, the colonists were predominantly English at the end of the century.

There was no census, but it is safe to say that by 1700 there were something like a quarter of a million settlers and descendants of settlers in the colonies. North of New England, French settlements were still little more than trading posts. South of the Carolinas, the Spanish presence on the Atlantic coast of North America was limited to isolated forts and missions. But in between—except for the sandy coast of New Jersey and the barren Eastern Shore of Maryland and Virginia—colonists were spread all along a 1,000-mile coastal strip that, at the time of the Pilgrims and the Jamestown settlers, had been virgin forest. About 80,000 lived in New England. Virginia, Maryland and the Carolinas had a total population of 85,000. The middle colonies—New York, New Jersey, Pennsylvania and Delaware—had 45,000.

In New England, the colonists still lived no more than 50 miles inland. In the South, plantations had spread as much as 150 miles from the sea coast, but they lay near deep tidewater rivers navigable by ships that would carry the tobacco crop to its overseas market. Everywhere, maritime commerce with Europe remained crucial. The largest and most prosperous settlements were seaports. By the end of the century, Boston had 7,000 inhabitants, New York 3,900. Providence, Philadelphia and Baltimore were all nearing city status. Even the plantation-minded South had a seaport city in Charleston.

And the maritime business of these ports was booming, for the mother country and the colonies had become dependent on each other's trade. In the 40-year period between 1660 and 1700, the value of annual English imports from the colonies doubled, going from about £200,000 to more than £400,000; and exports to the colonies rose from £105,000 to £350,000. Now that the issue of mere survival was past, a new sort of struggle would develop on the Atlantic and along the American littoral—the battle to determine whether the Old World or the New would control the profits of seagoing commerce.

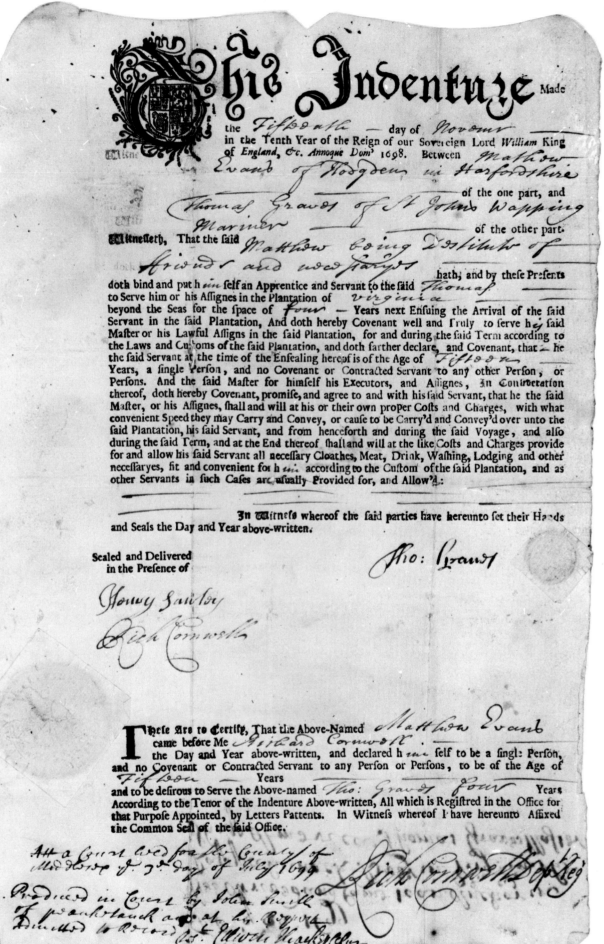

This Indenture Made
the _Fifteenth_ — day of _Novemr_
in the Tenth Year of the Reign of our Sovereign Lord _William_ King
of _England, &c. Annoque Dom'_ 1698. Between _Mathew_
Evans of Hodgden in Harfordshire
of the one part, and
Thomas Graves of St Johns Wapping
Mariner of the other part.

Witnesseth, That the said _Matthew being Destitute of_
friends and necessarys
hath; and by these Presents
doth bind and put himself an Apprentice and Servant to the said _Thomas_
to Serve him or his Assignes in the Plantation of _Virginia_
beyond the Seas for the space of _four_ — Years next Ensuing the Arrival of the said
Servant in the said Plantation, And doth hereby Covenant well and truly to serve he said
Master or his Lawful Assigns in the said Plantation, for and during the said Term according to
the Laws and Customs of the said Plantation, and doth farther declare, and Covenant, that he
the said Servant at the time of the Ensealing hereof is of the Age of _Fifteen_
Years, a single Person, and no Covenant or Contracted Servant to any other Person, or
Persons. And the said Master for himself his Executors, and Assignes, In Consideration
thereof, doth hereby Covenant, promise, and agree to and with his said Servant, that he the said
Master, or his Assignes, shall and will at his or their own proper Costs and Charges, with what
convenient Speed they may Carry and Convey, or cause to be Carry'd and Convey'd over unto the
said Plantation, his said Servant, and from henceforth and during the said Voyage, and also
during the said Term, and at the End thereof shall and will at the like Costs and Charges provide
for and allow his said Servant all necessary Cloathes, Meat, Drink, Washing, Lodging and other
necessaryes, fit and convenient for him according to the Custom of the said Plantation, and as
other Servants in such Cases are usually Provided for, and Allow'd:

In Witness whereof the said parties have hereunto set their Hands
and Seals the Day and Year above-written.

Sealed and Delivered
in the Presence of

Tho: Graves

Henry Sawley

Rich Cornwell

These Are to Certify, That the Above-Named _Matthew Evans_
came before Me _Richard Cornwell_, and declared himself to be a single Person,
and no Covenant or Contracted Servant to any Person or Persons, to be of the Age of
Fifteen Years
and to be desirous to Serve the Above-named _Tho: Graves four_ Years
According to the Tenor of the Indenture Above-written, All which is Registred in the Office for
that Purpose Appointed, by Letters Pattents. In Witness whereof I have hereunto Affixed
the Common Seal of the said Office.

Att a Court held for the County of
Middx ye 7th day of July 1699
Rich Cornwell Dept Regr

Produced in Court by John Smith

Early glimpses of the Indians' world

The American Indian was not altogether a stranger to the pioneers who came ashore at Jamestown and Plymouth. Many of them had seen their first Indians in engravings copied from the works of John White, a skilled painter who had accompanied some previous expeditions to the New World.

The English had begun to probe the North American continent with colonization in mind as early as 1584, when Sir Walter Raleigh dispatched an exploratory party under Captain Arthur Barlowe. White may have been a member of the expedition, though the records are unclear. There is no doubt, however, of his presence on a second and larger expedition that went out in 1585 to reconnoiter the American coast south of the Chesapeake; he signed on as surveyor and artist of the enterprise.

When the expedition landed at Roanoke Island, off the coast of what is now North Carolina, White visited Algonquian villages for miles around, sketching everything from the way the Indians caught and cooked their fish to the charnel houses in which they preserved the remains of their chiefs. This wealth of imagery, translated into detailed watercolors after his return to England, was as much a testimony to the artist's energy and curiosity as it was a record of Indian ways.

White might have rested on that achievement, but his craving for adventure remained strong. He sought and won a commission as commander of a third expedition, aimed at founding a permanent city near the Chesapeake. With a fleet of three vessels he sailed from Plymouth on May 8, 1587. Among the 112 men, women and children colonists were some of White's own kin—his pregnant daughter Eleanor and her husband, Ananias Dare.

In July they reached Roanoke Island, and stopped to reprovision and water the ships. For White, about the only pleasant incident of the trip occurred there—the birth of his granddaughter Virginia Dare, the first English child to be born in America. By then, the travelers were weary, even mutinous, and they refused to proceed up the coast without additional supplies from England. White acceded to their demands and went back to fetch some.

He reached England in late 1587 only to find his nation arming for war with the Spanish Armada—a crisis that kept him from returning to Roanoke until 1590. A shock awaited him. There was no sign of the settlers he had left behind. "We sounded with a trumpet," he wrote sadly when he was homeward bound, "but we had no answere." Their fate remains a mystery.

But 75 of White's paintings survive as a rich legacy of England's introduction to the New World. Widely copied and published throughout Europe for more than 150 years, they helped to establish the indelible image of an abundant America that would lure a steady stream of emigrants across the Atlantic for generations to come.

The broyling of their fish ouer t[he] flame of fier.

Fish broil over an Indian fire in this watercolor by John White. The Carolina Indians cooked and ate fish as soon as it was caught—a surprise to the English, who normally cured fish for a later day.

A variety of fishing techniques are recorded in this scene: One man rakes the water at the stern of a dugout as his companions paddle the craft or tend an on-board fire meant to lure fish to the surface; two other Indians wade in shallow water with spears poised; and a fencelike weir traps a catch for collection later.

The manner of their fishing.

Their rype corne

Their greene corne

Corne newly sprong

Their sittinge at meate

The house wherin the Tombe of their Herounds standeth.

The place of solemne prayer

SECOTON

A Ceremony in their prayers with strange iestuns and songes dansing abowt posts carued on the topps lyke mens faces.

In a view of an Algonquian village called Secoton (opposite), White showed Indians eating in the open (center) and performing a ritual dance within a circle of posts (bottom right). Three cornfields exhibit the staggered plantings that yielded harvests all summer.

A palisade encircles the village of Pomeiooc, guarding it from enemy attack. Indians warred, wrote an English observer, "by sudden surprising one an other, most commonly about the dawning of the day, or moone light."

The Tombe of their Cheroūnes or cheife personages, their flesh clene taken of from the bones saue the skynn and heare of theire heads, wch flesh is dried and enfolded in matts laide at theire feete. their bones also being made dry ar couered wth deare skynns not altering their forme or proporōtion. With theire Kywash, which is an Image of woode keeping the deade.

The towne of Pomeiock and true forme of their howses, couered and enclosed some wth matts, and some wth barcks of trees. All compassed abowt wth smale poles stock thick together in stedd of a wall.

The bodies of 10 Algonquian chiefs killed in war lie on a rack in the village charnel house beneath the gaze of a squatting wooden idol (right). A resident priest tended the ceremonial fire and "mumbleth his prayers nighte and day," one of White's companions recorded.

Theire sitting at meate.

An Indian man and his wife eat hominy from a tray. Hominy was made by hulling and boiling the hard kernels of Indian corn; it quickly became the settlers' principal meal, with bits of fish and meat added in the Indian fashion.

The flyer.

An Algonquian medicine man, called
a "flyer" by White because of his winglike
gestures, performs a dance intended
to cure the sick. The pouch at his side
contains tobacco, thought by the
Indians to possess medicinal properties.

An Indian chief, wearing a copper
ornament on his chest, strikes a pose
that White and his companions
saw frequently. The "cheefe men," wrote
one of the English, "fold their armes
together as they walke, or as they talke one
with another, in signe of wisdome."

A cheife Herowan.

A chief's wife carries a large gourd while her daughter fondles a doll—a gift from the English explorers. Gourds of this size were frequently used to hold a brew consisting of water, ginger, cinnamon, and sometimes sassafras; the English found it "a pleasant liquor."

A painted warrior, wearing an animal tail as a hunting trophy, assumes a proud stance with his longbow. The English were impressed by the archery of the Indians, noting that they were very accurate at 40 yards and could shoot an arrow as far as 120 yards.

Chapter 2
Tug of war for maritime rights

O n a spring evening in 1680, a rather odd couple was rowed out to a narrow-sterned merchantman, the *Expectation*, which lay at anchor in Boston harbor. One of the visitors was a Massachusetts Bay Puritan named Joseph Webb; he held the title of marshal and carried himself with stiff-backed self-importance. The other member of the twosome could be identified half the harbor away as an Englishman—a fellow of "modish nic-nacs, dagger and perriwigg," an observer wrote. The stylish gentleman was Edward Randolph and, as the King's collector of customs, he was even more puffed up by his office than the marshal.

Believing that the *Expectation* had been engaged in smuggling, he had tried to inspect her cargo the night before, but was sent on his way with rude Yankee threats of a dunking and other such rough treatment. Now, having enlisted Webb's support, Randolph returned to the ship armed with a governor's warrant that empowered him to board her. The only thing he had forgotten was chalk. The oarsman fished in his pocket and found a piece. Randolph took it, clambered onto the *Expectation's* deck and marked a broad arrow on the mast. By that sign he seized the errant merchantman for the Crown.

The chalk mark was second only to the flag as a token of royal possession. Throughout England's New World colonies, it had been used to claim land, virgin timber and other sorts of property for the King. With his stroke on the mast of the *Expectation*, Randolph signaled the beginning of an English effort to gain firm control over one of the greatest colonial assets of all—America's merchant marine.

In the 60 years that had passed since the landing of the *Mayflower*, the flow of goods to and from the New World had increased spectacularly. In the Southern colonies, 46,000 acres were devoted to growing tobacco for overseas consumers. In the North, 34 shipyards were constructing whole fleets of vessels to conduct all manner of trade. Moreover, colonial merchants, no longer content simply to produce exports for shipment to England, were building commercial networks that bypassed the mother country entirely. Randolph wrote to his superiors back in London: "It is the great care of the merchants to keep their ships in constant employ, which makes them trye all ports to force a trade." So common was the sight of colonial ships in the Caribbean, Randolph added, that "there is little left for the merchants residing in England to import into any of the plantations."

Another British visitor had earlier written home that the colonists "look upon themselves as a free state, there being many against owing

Two square-riggers and an assortment of sloops and schooners crowd the basin of a small shipyard on Gray's Inn Creek in the Chesapeake Bay area of Maryland. Such shipyards proliferated throughout the 18th Century; between 1730 and 1760 the ratio of American-built vessels employed by British merchants climbed from 1 out of every 6 to 1 of 4.

the king, or having any dependence on England." A little later a member of the Massachusetts General Court, the legislature by which the Crown allowed the colonists some limited self-government, went so far as to claim that "the laws of England are bounded by within the fower seas, and do not reach America. The subjects of his majestie here being not represented in Parliament, so we have not looked at ourselves to be impeded in our trade by them." In London a government official responded that, unless this sort of thinking was discouraged, "there can be nothing expected but a total breach."

Talk of a breach was rare and would not be taken seriously until well into the next century. But by the time Edward Randolph appeared on the scene, England had already defined its position in no uncertain terms: Between 1651 and 1696, Parliament passed a series of Navigation Acts that were designed to shape colonial sea traffic to suit the interests of the mother country. The Acts compelled the colonists to send certain "enumerated commodities" only to England or to other English colonies. At first, the listed commodities were limited to sugar, tobacco, cotton, indigo and dyewoods; later, practically all colonial commodities—from whalebone to lumber—would be included. A 5 per cent tax was imposed on the enumerated exports.

As for imports, the Acts stipulated that virtually all goods had to come into the colonies on "English vessels navigated by Englishmen." Colonial vessels qualified as English, but any cargo that was brought in on the vessel of another nation was liable to "forfeiture." To further tighten the hold on colonial imports, Parliament insisted that cargoes originating in other European countries had to pass through England, where duties were paid on the goods; any ship's captain violating this stricture could be arrested for smuggling.

For England, the Navigation Acts were a bonanza. Between 1660 and 1688, its merchant shipping doubled, and England emerged as the undisputed leader in world trade, passing the Netherlands, which had held that position for half a century. English businessmen financed the finest ships then afloat, paying top prices and outdoing the Dutch in working out credit arrangements with overseas suppliers of various commodities. As a direct consequence of the trade laws, London became Europe's greatest entrepôt; throughout the next century, England would transship to other countries four fifths of the tobacco it received from the American South and three quarters of the rice.

The colonies, too, benefited from the Navigation Acts. The Southern planters were awarded a monopoly on the shipment of tobacco to England and thus had a guaranteed market for their products. Another boon was a surge in the already thriving colonial shipbuilding industry. Because England had used up its own timber and had no sources closer than the Baltic, it turned to the colonies, where timber abounded on every hand. Some Englishmen journeyed across the Atlantic to oversee the industry; Thomas Coram, a London philanthropist and merchant, found a "vast great plenty of oak and fir Timber" at the tiny settlement of Taunton, Massachusetts, and between 1697 and 1702 personally supervised a shipyard there. "If ever a Stop should be put to the Building of Ships in New England," wrote another London merchant, Joshua Gee, a

English entrepreneur Thomas Coram sits beside a globe that symbolizes his activities on both sides of the Atlantic. He ardently promoted the settlement of English, Scottish, French and German emigrants in colonies from Nova Scotia to Georgia—and made a fortune supplying English shipyards with the tar, pitch and hemp that the colonies produced.

few years later, "we should soon sink in our Navigations and those of the Dutch flourish in its former Height and Grandeur."

Many of the vessels built in these shipyards were owned or chartered by colonists, and the trading profits they generated were the basis for some handsome personal fortunes. When Randolph first visited America in 1676, thirty merchants in Massachusetts alone were worth between £10,000 and £20,000. Foremost among them was a trader named Philip English—a man whose energy and vision were complemented by a less-than-respectful view of the mercantile policies of the mother country. He was, in fact, a perfect example of why England felt threatened by the commercial practices of its progeny across the Atlantic.

Philip English was born Phillippe L'Anglois on the Channel Island of Jersey. Not much is known of his youth except that, like most Channel Islanders, he took to the sea as a young man. By 1660 or so, he rose to be master of his own ship, and sometime before 1670 he came to the New World, settled in Salem, Massachusetts, and anglicized his name. But he kept his Old World ties, rather as if the Atlantic were only a slightly wider English Channel. Those diverse ties were the secret to his success. Starting out with only a ketch—a two-master, with square sails on the foremast and a fore-and-aft rig on the mainmast—he would carry any cargo anywhere and trade it for almost anything else, whether or not the Navigation Acts allowed it.

First of all, there was fish. "Fish," wrote an early member of the Massachusetts Bay colony, "is the only great stapple which the Country produceth for forraine parts and is so benefitiall for making returns for what wee need." A Marblehead fisherman—a contemporary of Philip English's—upbraided a too-zealous preacher with the statement that "our ancestors came not here for religion. Their main end was to catch fish." English bought fish from men who harvested the nearby waters, and carried it to the Southern colonies—along with quantities of rum, cider, wooden bowls, platters, pails, kegs and a variety of other goods that New Englanders produced. In exchange, he brought back wheat, pork and tobacco. He also ventured to the West Indies to fetch sugar and molasses (for making rum), and he voyaged across the Atlantic to the French ports of St. Malo, Nantes, La Rochelle and Bordeaux, where he traded his various New World acquisitions for vinegar, linen, silk, stockings, coats, wine and an array of other Continental products.

To make his business truly cosmopolitan, this resourceful Salem merchant-captain financed his activities with foreign capital. In 1677, for example, he signed a contract at St. Malo with an agent of a certain Sire Moise Coubel. For the sum of £208, put up by Coubel, English agreed to conduct a circuitous trading journey: He would first sail from St. Malo to Boston; from there he would proceed to Bilbao in Spain, to Bordeaux, to a series of ports in England, and finally back to St. Malo, where Coubel would collect 30 per cent on his investment. Even at that high rate of interest, English could expect to end up with a sizable profit.

He arranged countless such ventures, prospering mightily. By 1692 he had acquired 21 vessels, a wharf and 14 buildings in Salem; one of the buildings, a mansion on Essex Street, projected porches like so many prows, with two upper stories overhanging the street. It was spoken of

with reverence as "English's Great House." That year, however, his empire building was momentarily checked—not because of his frequent flouting of the law in his business affairs but because of witch-hunting hysteria. The mania began in February, when several young Salem girls, including the daughter and niece of the local minister, began acting strangely, writhing on the floor and crying out in pain. Their mysterious affliction quickly spread to other girls and young women. Doctors were puzzled, but not Cotton Mather, a fiery Puritan minister and self-proclaimed expert on witchcraft. "An army of devils is horribly broke in upon Salem," he declared, "and the houses of the good people there are filled with doleful shrieks of their children and servants, tormented by invisible hands, with torture altogether preternatural."

Along with hundreds of other men and women, Philip English's wife was accused of witchcraft and arrested. After she had been confined for six weeks in a chamber of a public house while awaiting trial, English himself was accused. With the assistance of some of their friends, the couple fled to New York. They stayed there a year, until the hysteria had passed, then returned home to Salem. A celebration was held in their honor, and English took command of his commercial empire again, directing it until his death in 1736.

To the end, his freewheeling mercantile style was never curbed. Late

In a secluded Newfoundland cove, 18th Century fishermen cure and dry their cod catches from the nearby Grand Banks. In the opening decade of the century an estimated 35,000 fishermen from England and France made annual expeditions across the Atlantic to fish in North America—only to meet increasing competition from colonists, who wanted a share in the harvest for themselves.

in life, in written instructions to a captain who was taking a cargo of fish to the West Indies, he said, "Make Returne in yr Vessel or any other for Salem in such Goods as you shall see best, and if you see Cause to take a freight to any port . . . , I lieve it with your Best Conduct, Managem't or Care for my best advantage. So please God to give you a prosperous voyage, I remain yr Friend and Owner."

Philip English's trading activities were notable chiefly for their scale. Many other New England merchants had the same business philosophy—diversity in goods, diversity in ports, and a refusal to comply with the regulations imposed by Parliament. In the end, the issue of what America could aspire to in the way of seagoing commerce was to be resolved only by revolution. But that would be a long time coming. For a good part of the 17th and 18th Centuries, the contest had the wild exuberance of an adolescent-and-parent conflict. Ingenious young Yankee Doodle, sailing for his profit margin, matched tricks with stubborn old John Bull, trying to deny him his revenue.

No royal harasser enraged the colonial traders more than that man in the rowboat, Edward Randolph. He was the personification of one of life's most unwelcome figures, the tax collector, and to the colonists he was all the more galling in that he was not one of themselves.

Randolph would seem to have been born to swim against the tide. He came from a landed family; some of his kin owned farms south and southeast of Canterbury. But his father, a physician, had been a younger son and in accordance with the law of primogeniture inherited almost nothing. Throughout his life, Randolph displayed some of the petulance of a dispossessed heir. His attitude toward the colonists was almost personal, as if he saw them getting away with what was rightly his as an Englishman.

At the age of 18, he entered Gray's Inn, one of the four ancient Inns of Court, where Englishmen prepared to be barristers. Randolph stayed less than a year, and he never practiced at the bar. But a legalistic view of the world was never to leave him. Early in his career, he devoted his energies to a tangled and protracted lawsuit over the possession of cattle, the rights to pasturage and the proceeds of an annuity. Even his first Atlantic crossing was made in pursuit of a legal matter: He sailed for the New World in 1676 on behalf of a cousin, Robert Mason, who claimed proprietary rights to territory in New Hampshire. England's Lords of Trade decided that, as long as Randolph was there, he could look about and report to them on what he learned of the economic and military strength of the colonies.

The Lords had happened on the perfect agent—the supreme bureaucrat. Only a man who possessed a zealous devotion to a book of regulations could have believed in the possibility of thoroughly yoking colonial commerce—and that was the ultimate duty to which Randolph's somewhat self-defined commission led him. After just one month in America, he was convinced that the spirit and the letter of the Navigation Acts had been violated to the point "whereby his Majestie is damaged in his Customs above £100,000 yearely." By the end of his stay, Randolph had compiled a detailed 25-page report on the state of affairs

in New England, which he submitted to a Parliamentary Committee for Trade and Plantations.

Randolph's report touched off a series of debates in Parliament. The Lords of Trade maintained that England could hope to hold the colonists in check only by revoking the Massachusetts Bay colony's charter, which granted the colonists the right to elect their own governors and the freedom to make many sorts of laws without interference from the Crown. Randolph argued that the governor should hold office by royal appointment instead and that the laws the colonists made should be sent to London for approval.

The charter remained in force, but Randolph returned to Boston in 1680—this time carrying a royal commission as the collector, surveyor and searcher of customs for the New England colonies. Not surprisingly, he found himself an unpopular, if not hated, figure. "I am received at Boston more like a spy than one of his majesty's servants," he wrote. Indeed, a Boston poet had a few salvos ready for him:

> Welcome, Sir, welcome from the easterne shore,
> With a commission stronger than before
> To play the horse-leach; robb us of our Fleeces,
> To rend our land, and teare it all to pieces:
> Randolph's returned, that hector,
> Confirm'd at home to be the sharp Collector.

An elderly man vainly protests his innocence during a Salem witchcraft trial in 1692. Among the hundreds accused of being witches or wizards was shipowner Philip English, who fled to New York. Twenty men and women were executed.

Unfazed by his reception, Randolph proceeded about his business and challenged the *Expectation*. He went on to seize 36 more vessels in the next three years, prosecuting their captains for various violations of the Navigation Acts. But he could not sway the merchant-dominated colonial courts, and all but two of the captains caught in his efficient net were acquitted. Randolph was driven apoplectic with frustration. Yet he seems never to have thought of quitting. Back and forth across the Atlantic he shuttled, now cooling his heels patiently in the outer offices of Whitehall, where he sought writs to serve on the upstart colonists; now pushing the royal Governors in the colonies to grant him more power.

In 1685 his fondest hopes were realized. Parliament, by now fed up with colonial waywardness, revoked the New England charters, and Randolph was issued a commission to be secretary and sole registrar of the newly formed Dominion of New England, which was to be controlled from London. The new government would allow New Englanders to continue to elect their own governors, but their selections would be subject to royal review. The militia would serve under officers of the Crown. And all land would be owned by the King, to whom the colonists would have to pay rent. The new arrangement naturally caused extreme dismay in the colonies. "This Monday we begin palpably to die," Samuel Sewall, one of Boston's leading citizens, wrote in his diary.

Only two weeks after the Dominion was established, Randolph sent a report to England that three ships had been condemned for smuggling. It looked as if the Navigation Acts would be enforced at last. But now, curiously, Randolph was caught in a trap of his own devising: His relentless policing of the ports had a dampening effect on colonial prosperity. As customs inspectors began to make a thorough search of every ship upon arrival, New England was unable to bring in goods that had originated outside the mother country. With less money changing hands (albeit illegally), the local economy weakened, and the colonists were less able to afford legal shipments from England. One of the King's counselors reported that a related act, which prohibited New Englanders from fishing off French Nova Scotia, had caused a depression in that industry. "Heavy Impositions on Sugar and Tobacco," he added, had hurt the Southern colonies. "This country is poor," he concluded; "the exact execution of the acts of trade hath much impoverished them."

In 1689 the English throne passed to William of Orange, a nobleman who had championed the Netherlanders' fight for freedom from the Spanish Crown. The American colonists, believing that the new monarch would be sympathetic to their grievances, rebelled against the Dominion; mobs seized the royal Governor and Edward Randolph and clapped both of them in prison. Randolph, writing home from there, sarcastically gave his address as "the common jail in New Algiers."

Contrary to expectations, King William did not restore the terms of the old charter, and he commanded the colonists to release the Governor and Randolph. After spending eight months in jail, Randolph left Massachusetts on a merchantman bound for London. The final document he signed before departing was a voucher for four pounds one shilling—the bill for his meals while in prison.

New England was quit at last of Randolph's prickly interference,

Tender care for the golden leaf

Engravings from a study of tobacco culture published in 1800 demonstrate how the leaf was prepared for shipment.

Almost any commodity that was transported across the Atlantic in the early 1600s faced some risk of damage during the 3,000-mile voyage. But tobacco—first exported in 1613 from Jamestown—was subject to more shipping problems than most. Rough handling could bruise the fragile leaves, reducing their value in England. Worse still, tobacco was prey to mold in damp holds; during the early years of the tobacco trade, whole shiploads of the colonial leaf spoiled en route to market.

Within a few decades, however, the colonists developed curing and packing techniques that greatly reduced losses. These methods—pictured at left and keyed by numbers—changed little over the next 200 years, although the painstaking work was gradually transferred from the growers to indentured servants and slaves.

To reduce the risk of rot, the tobacco was dried in stages. After harvest, the stalks were placed on scaffolds (1) and left briefly in the sun. They were then hung up inside barnlike "tobacco houses" (2) for about a month, until they had lost most of their moisture but were not yet brittle.

As a first step in packing, the leaves were stripped from the stalks and then wrapped in small bundles, or "hands" (3). These were laboriously crammed into wooden hogsheads, a layer at a time; each layer was compressed by means of a weighted lever (4). In addition to reducing the tobacco's volume for stowage, compression forced the tobacco into a solid mass that was remarkably resistant to mold and moisture in leaky holds.

When filled, the hogsheads were delivered to public warehouses (5) for storage until they could be inspected (6). Inferior tobacco was burned; tobacco that passed inspection was conveyed to port.

The colonists devised creative ways to haul the heavy hogsheads from one place to another. If the destination could be reached by water, the planters freighted the casks in twin canoes, joined together with crossbeams for stability (7). Otherwise, they carted the casks in wagons or turned the hogsheads on their sides, hitched them to horses and rolled them overland (8)— a method that had a secondary benefit of leveling rough trails into superior routes called "tobacco roads." At the wharf, the planters generally sold the tobacco to an agent of a British merchant, who arranged for its passage.

Careful preparation of the tobacco assured merchants of its quality; the merchants, in turn, guaranteed Southern planters a market for virtually all the tobacco that they could produce. By 1775, Virginia and Maryland were earning 75 per cent of their export incomes from sales of the "golden leaf."

In a 16th Century woodcut, Nicotiana tabacum is depicted alongside an oversized cigar made from twisted tobacco leaves. The plant, native to South America, was first brought to Europe by the Spaniards. In 1612, colonist John Rolfe carried seeds from the plant to Virginia, whose soil and temperate climate proved an ideal environment.

As merchants hover in attendance, slaves ready hogsheads for weighing and loading on a ship bound for England.

but the sister colonies were not. In 1692, Randolph sailed across the Atlantic again, this time for James City, as the capital of Virginia was now styled, to investigate the commerce of Virginia (and, while he was at it, neighboring Maryland and Pennsylvania as well). He found a different way of life and a different manner of trade—but affairs no more to his liking than before.

Unlike their fellow colonists to the north, the Virginians had not taken to seafaring. They had not been compelled to do so, because English merchants sent their own agents across the ocean to obtain the tobacco that was yielded in such abundance by the fertile soil. The Crown was in on the operation from start to finish, lending money to the planters, controlling the narrow entrance of Chesapeake Bay to keep foreign vessels out, and assigning British men-of-war to protect tobacco ships from predation by England's enemies.

A homely triumph of American shipbuilding

For **LIVERPOOL,**
(To fail in a Month)
THE Ship BRILLIANT, WILLIAM PRIESTMAN Mafter; can take in 200 Hogfheads of Tobacco on Freight, with Liberty of Confignment. For Terms apply to JOHN LAURENCE, & Co.
☞ Who have alfo FOR CHARTER, a SHIP of 400 Hogfheads, and a BRIG of 8000 Bufhels Burthen.
NORFOLK, *June* 6, 1775.

To judge from appearances, *Brilliant* was hardly a fitting name for the plain little ship whose maiden voyage was perfunctorily noted in the 1775 advertisement above. Stodgy in profile and broad of beam (right), she was typical rather than exceptional—one of hundreds of vessels that ferried cargoes between America and England in the 18th Century. But the *Brilliant* represented the shipwright's art at its finest—and the coming of age of the all-important colonial industry of shipbuilding.

Colonists had no sooner settled on the American seaboard than they began constructing ships. Convenience combined with necessity to encourage the practice; timber was plentiful and sturdy, and the least difficult route of transportation between one isolated settlement and another was by water. By 1676, some 730 craft had been built in Massachusetts alone, and more were being built in shipyards dotting the coast from the Kennebec River in Maine to Chesapeake Bay in Virginia.

The earliest vessels were small pinnaces and shallops for coastal cruising. But England's growing appetite for New World resources created a demand for larger, oceangoing ships. By the early 18th Century some colonial vessels reached 350 tons. The biggest of them could stow more than 13,000 bushels of grain or 700 tobacco hogsheads—the four-foot-high barrels that, when packed with tobacco leaf, weighed nearly half a ton each. The ships themselves became highly desirable merchandise abroad; by 1760, one third of the tonnage sailing under the British flag had been built in the colonies—at a lower cost than was possible in Europe, and also with a keen regard for quality.

Among those ships was the *Brilliant*, a tobacco packet whose plans survive through a twist of fate that had nothing to do with her builder. When she took on her first cargo at Norfolk in the summer of 1775, the Revolution was already under way in New England, and Virginia's leaders, threatening to join the rebellion, had ordered an embargo on tobacco shipments to England as of September. The *Brilliant* became part of a large, hurriedly assembled convoy that carried to the mother country the last shipment of colonial tobacco—a record 100 million pounds.

That was the end of her career as a tobacco packet. In England the Admiralty bought her from her British owner, carefully recorded her dimensions and equipment, and then converted her into a warship. After the Revolution, she was converted again, this time into a whaler. In that guise, she battled the North Atlantic for 15 more years under the British flag.

The Revolution decimated the American storehouse of ships because most of them suffered the fate of the *Brilliant*—purchase or seizure by the British Admiralty. But builders of ships like her stood ready to carry on—and to bring about a flowering of the American merchant marine in the century ahead.

The planter, meanwhile, had no worry except growing the crop—a simple supervisory matter, since one indentured laborer could tend 10,000 plants from seed to harvest—and transporting it to a waterfront warehouse somewhere upriver from Chesapeake Bay. If he lived by a river himself, as the earliest planters invariably did, he reached the warehouse by barge. If time and prosperity had taken his plantation inland, he moved the leaf overland by an ingenious method: His hogsheads—the massive barrels used to hold the tobacco —were fitted with axle-like protrusions and rolled over the gentle Virginia hills by teams of oxen or horses. At the warehouse the visiting agents bought full cargoes at a time and consigned them to English ships that waited in the Chesapeake. With his profits the planter purchased goods that the English agents had brought along with them—anything from wigs to harpsichords.

This view of the three-masted square-rigger Brilliant was drawn from a detailed description made by the Royal Navy in 1776. She was 75 feet long at the keel, had a cargo capacity of 285 tons and was built of Virginia pine, oak and cedar.

The Southern colonists also produced a number of commodities need-ed by England for naval stores—tar, pitch, resin and turpentine from the woodlands. Toward the end of the 17th Century they found another profitable undertaking—cultivating rice, a grain that was particularly congenial to the Southern swamplands—and a little later they took up raising the plant that yielded indigo, a dyestuff that would be much in demand by English merchants as the development of textile machinery accelerated. Both products would, like tobacco and naval stores, bring English merchants to their threshold.

Even if the Southerners left maritime conveyance to others, they ex-hibited a good deal of skill in evading the Navigation Acts. Randolph, surveying his first tobacco fleet as it collected the crop from all the creeks and bays of the Chesapeake and made rendezvous off Old Point Comfort, Virginia, counted a convoy of 120 sail. In theory, the Crown would receive handsome revenues from such a quantity of exports. But Ran-dolph soon discovered a marked pattern of negligence among the cus-toms agents responsible for collecting the tobacco duty; they were quite willing to forget about the Crown's revenues so long as they received suitable under-the-table compensation themselves.

Randolph composed still another report for the London authorities—"an account of severall things whereby illegal Trade is encouraged in Virginia, Maryland, and Pennsylvania." The evidence suggested that about £50,000 in tobacco tax was lost annually from Virginia alone. Randolph was no more able to enforce the law there, however, than he had been in Massachusetts.

The indefatigable tax collector sailed to America for the last time in the summer of 1702. He was then in his 71st year. As unbending as ever, he seized the ship on which he was traveling for some minor violation of the Navigation Acts. The case, as usual, was lost in court. A few months after reaching his destination in Maryland, he died. At the time, the cash in his possession amounted to a pitiful 2 pounds 11 shillings. The inven-tory of his personal belongings consisted for the most part of a long list of secondhand clothes: an old silk nightgown and sash, a black suit of clothes, a silk vest, two hats, a pair of breeches, and so on.

Edward Randolph's life had had a magnificent futility to it. He was a brilliant nuisance—a tirelessly fussy chaperon of traders' rendezvous. But in the end, he could no more control the comings and goings of colonial seafarers than he could control the sea itself. He was the stone breakwater over whom the Yankee traders finally smashed.

By the time Randolph died, America's Atlantic seaboard had the fastest growing population of any place on the globe. Emigrants continued to make the fearsome ocean crossing—not only English now, but Scotch-Irish from Ulster, Highlanders from Scotland, Welsh, some Irish, consid-erable numbers of Germans from the Rhine Valley, Dutch, Swiss, Swedes, Jews from all over Europe and slaves from West Africa. The population of the colonies stood at around a quarter of a million in 1700; with emigration and natural growth the figure was to double, redouble and redouble again, to more than two million in the second half of the 18th Century. By 1774 there would be 20,000 people living in Boston,

DELVALLE's Beſt Virginia *TOBACCO* in LONDON.

*"Best Virginia" tobacco is touted
on these labels, which London merchants
applied to tobacco cartons in the mid-
18th Century. Not everyone welcomed the
new product; noting that many taverns
and coffeehouses catered exclusively to
smokers, one critic wondered why "people
should leave their own firesides to
sit in the midst of eternal fog and stench."*

30,000 in New York and 40,000 in Philadelphia. As early as 1690, Boston could claim the distinction of being the third largest port in the world, after London and Bristol.

Of all the people who came to seek a new life in the colonies, none fared better than those with a taste for commerce. A merchant, as the lexicographer Samuel Johnson defined him in the 18th Century, was "one who trafficks to remote countries." In America, the merchants were that and something more. They were the retailers and wholesalers of the goods they imported. They invested in sawmills and gristmills, breweries and distilleries, iron foundries, new buildings, shipyards and wharves. They were the colonies' largest employers and chief lenders. The British, in order to keep control of currency, forbade the existence of banks in America, but the merchants became bankers by virtue of holding bills of exchange and I.O.U.s on the goods they dealt in. They also became brokers in a business that was then in its infancy—insurance. In return for a fee, they promised their clients that they would make good on the full value of any cargo that failed to reach its destination.

The threats to seagoing commerce were greater than they had ever been. In the late 17th and early 18th Centuries, pirates operated all along the colonial coast, lurking in coves and bays, and racing out to seize a merchant ship as soon as she was spotted on the horizon. The pirates would then sell the cargo in the nearest port and split the profits among themselves. Some of them—Captain William Kidd and Edward Teach, known as Blackbeard—attained celebrity among the colonists; they occasionally walked the streets of Boston, New York and Charleston with impunity, spending their gold coins. Eventually the British sent out warships and saw to it that pirates were hanged.

Privateering—a legalized form of piracy—was a more prevalent and long-lasting threat. Only a thin line separated outlawed freebooters from privateers—captains of merchantmen who in wartime were licensed by the Crown to seize the ships of enemy nations, or any vessel sailing for, or trading with, an enemy nation. (The term "privateer" also applied to ships engaged in this quasi-military activity.) The license, known as a letter of marque, required the captain to turn over the captured ship and a percentage of her cargo to his government; the rest was divided among the officers, crew, himself and the shipowner.

Between 1652 and 1763, England engaged in seven wars with the Netherlands, France and Spain. During all those conflicts, every colonial vessel was at the mercy of the ships of England's enemies. But if her captain turned to privateering, the game was even; moreover, the captain could hope to realize far greater profits from plundering than he could from routine trading. Not surprisingly, the legalized piracy expanded apace. In September of 1744 the Boston *Weekly Post-Boy* reported: "'Tis computed there will be before winter one hundred and thirteen sail of privateers at sea from the British-American colonies, most stout vessels and well manned. A naval force, some say, equal that of Great Britain in the time of Queen Elizabeth." During the nine-year French and Indian War fought in the 1750s and 1760s, an estimated 11,000 Americans sailed on privateering vessels.

Typically such a vessel measured about 200 tons and was armed with

German emigrants in a strange new land

During the 18th Century, as many as 200,000 German Protestants left their homeland and emigrated to America, via England, rather than yield to a revived Catholicism in Germany. Some of them settled in the colony of Georgia, founded by a group of humanitarian Englishmen in 1732 to serve as a refuge for unfortunates of all kinds.

Little is known of their early efforts to take root in the Georgian wilderness—with a singular exception. Philip Georg Friedrich von Reck, a young nobleman who recruited Protestants for the colony, found time to document his labors in words and pictures. His chronicle conveys a sense of adventure that must have been shared by countless emigrants.

In 1734 and again in 1736, von Reck escorted groups of Germans across the Atlantic on English ships to the environs of present-day Savannah. There, they laid out a settlement they called Ebenezer—a Biblical name meaning "rock of life." Two years later they moved the settlement a few miles upriver, and called it New Ebenezer.

New Ebenezer flourished, managing to export creditable quantities of rice, indigo and hemp. But the divisiveness of the American Revolution spelled the settlement's doom. Some of the residents still felt such gratitude to England, under whose auspices they had found refuge from persecution, that they informed on their neighbors rather than join the fight for independence. Many of the informed-upon left to resettle elsewhere.

When the war ended, New Ebenezer was a ghost town. All that survived of its first bright hopes was a series of finely rendered sketches by von Reck. He had intended these views—many of them accompanied by handwritten notes—to lure additional settlers.

Von Reck himself had lingered in Georgia less than a year. He migrated to Denmark, where he served in a government post until the age of 82. His manuscript had meanwhile been published, but without the drawings. The sketches' whereabouts remained unknown for two centuries—until they turned up in the Royal Library in Copenhagen in 1976.

The vessel London Merchant carefully makes her way past the Isle of Wight (1) as she follows the Symonds through a narrow channel between the rock formation known as the Needles (2) and shoal water (3). Together, the two ships transported 257 colonists to Georgia, where each family was given a small town lot with a garden plot and up to 50 acres of land.

A notation in German at the top of this sketch identifies these as "the first huts and shelters in Ebenezer." The colonists—many of them wearing the broad-brimmed hats traditional in their homeland—have finished clearing the riverfront and are hard at work on two large communal buildings.

Supply boats land at New Ebenezer on the Savannah River. The town was the second established by the German emigrants, and rather than start from scratch, they dismantled the homes they had built at the previous site and transported the pieces five miles upriver.

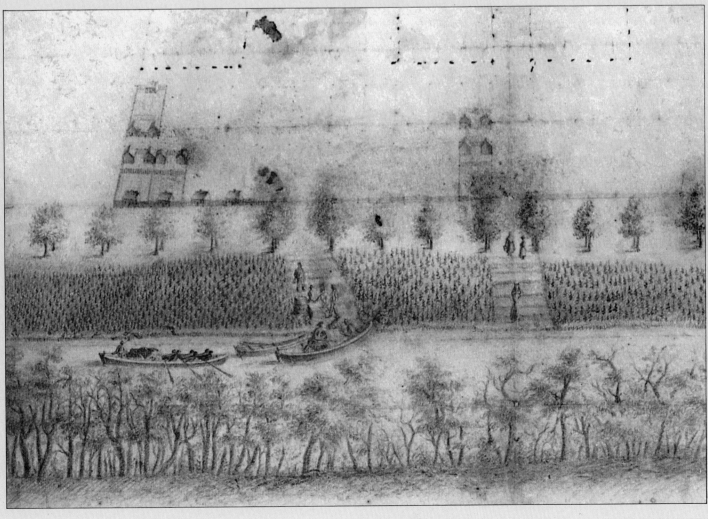

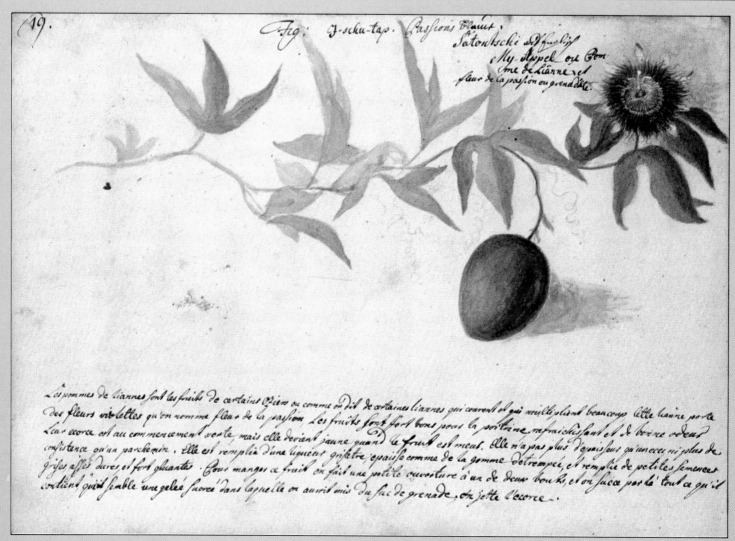

The showy blossoms and sweet fruit of the passionflower fascinated von Reck. His description was copied from a French reference book.

The tasty squash was cultivated in many of New Ebenezer's gardens.

Von Reck enthusiastically rated watermelon "the best of all melons."

about 18 cannon, which might be as large as the 6-pounders on men-of-war. She carried perhaps 100 men. Some were ordinary seamen, but many were adventurers who were taken on simply because they knew how to fight. All were armed with pistols, muskets, cutlasses, and grenade-like bombs that were hurled by hand.

A privateer followed a convoy at a safe distance, not striking until the ships were spread out by a gale or a fog. Warships that escorted the merchantmen rarely gave pursuit; the quick sailing and sharpshooting of privateers made it too dangerous. In 1746 an unusually large, 380-ton American privateer, the *Prince Charles*, came upon the *Rising Sun*, an equally large and well-armed French vessel that had strayed from her convoy. The *Prince Charles's* captain disguised his men as marines by issuing grenadier caps, and the *Rising Sun*, thinking that she had been set upon by a man-of-war, promptly surrendered. By her captain's guile, the *Prince Charles* captured a cargo that included 1,117 hogsheads of sugar and 458 casks of coffee. A common seaman, who normally earned less than two pounds a month, might fetch more than £100 as his share of such a prize.

On occasion, a privateering venture had gentlemanly overtones. In 1745 the New York privateer the *Clinton* arrived in her home port with a modest prize—a 14-gun, 180-ton Spanish sloop, the *Pamona*, carrying 88 casks of sugar, 237 casks of indigo and 15 bales of cotton. The captain of the *Pamona* was so impressed by the fact that the attackers had refrained from robbing his men of their personal possessions that he treated the privateers to a gala feast in New York featuring a roasted ox.

Clashes could also be fierce and bloody. In January of 1758 the American privateer *Thruloe*, carrying 84 men and 14 guns, fought a close-range battle against the French privateer *Les Deux Amis*, with 98 men and 10 guns. An old record says that "it was not until three hundred powder flasks and seventy-two stinkpots" had been thrown on the decks of *Les Deux Amis* that the French ship surrendered. Thirty-seven of the Americans, and 80 of the French, had been killed or badly wounded.

It took imagination and no little daring to engage in an occupation that was fraught with so many hazards as transatlantic shipping. But to the men who dared and succeeded, the rewards were inestimable. Their money gave them power; their boldness gave them celebrity.

In the 18th Century one of the most successful and celebrated of all was Thomas Hancock, founder of an eminent merchant family. A Puritan minister's son, Hancock grew up in the Massachusetts town of Lexington. In 1717, at the age of 14, he took himself to Boston and signed on as an apprentice to a bookseller. Seven years later, he went into the book trade on his own. Since almost all books sold in America were printed in England, the business automatically made him an importer, an activity that was much to his taste. Soon Hancock was pushing books to the back shelves and stocking his store with such English manufactures as cloth and cutlery. To finance additional imports, he began looking around for something he could export as well.

One ill-fated venture involved shipping locally written theological tracts to the English; the overseas reading public was decidedly uninter-

The fruit of the satapi, or papaw, soothed stomach-aches.

Flying squirrels were easily caught—and turned into a favorite New Ebenezer soup.

ested. That failure hardly slowed Hancock down, however. He spied trading opportunities in all directions. England needed whale oil (for lamps and lubrication) and whalebone (to stiffen corsets, helmets and whips); the New England settlements needed West Indies hemp and rum; the West Indies needed New York and New Jersey beef, dairy products and grains; southern Europe needed cured fish; colonists all along the Atlantic coast had acquired a taste for tea. The list ran on and on, and soon Hancock's ships and agents seemed to be everywhere, engaged in ever more intricate cycles of commercial exchange.

Hancock, like the merchants whom Randolph had tussled with in the previous century, readily succumbed to the temptation to disregard the Navigation Acts and trade directly with non-English ports whenever it was to his advantage. Naturally this called for some sleight of hand in bringing goods home. On one occasion when a vessel approached Boston harbor with a cargo of Spanish lemons, Hancock sent out a message telling the captain to "divide them out before you Come up to Town." Such a ploy was no doubt routine.

Frequently Hancock ordered his captains to return from England by way of Dutch Surinam on the northern coast of South America, or the Dutch West Indies island of St. Eustatius. Dealing with the Dutch anywhere was antithetical to the policies of the mother country, and Han-

The bustling port of Boston, center of American commerce during the 18th Century, is ringed by church steeples and a visiting English fleet in this 1773 engraving by silversmith and patriot Paul Revere. Grandest of the dozens of wharves along the crowded waterfront is Long Wharf (center), which extended half a mile into the harbor and was linked on its landward side with the city's marketplace at Faneuil Hall.

cock had to caution his captains against giving any hint of where they had been: "Observe when you come on to our Coasts," he wrote one of his captains, "not to Speak with any Vessells nor let any of your men write up to their wives when you arrive at our light house."

By 1740, Hancock had ventured into direct trade with the Netherlands. He put a pair of ships, the *Three Friends* and the *Charming Lydia* (named after his wife), on a triangular route bounded by Boston, the West Indies and Amsterdam. The ships would take West Indies sugar to Holland, then load up with tea and paper, and sail straight for home. The cargoes would be unloaded in Massachusetts ports that were not covered by customs officers, and the ships would then proceed to Boston with only ballast to show the inspectors. In 1742 as one of his captains was about to set off for Amsterdam, Hancock instructed him that, on the return trip, he should "neither bring so much as a Letter for anybody here, but what shall come under Cover to me and be Carefull that your people bring no Letters neither for any one. And speak with nobody upon your Passage if you can possibly help it."

If Hancock was furtive about bringing in his well-laden ships, he was quite the opposite about his personal life. With a panache that would

At the entrance to Boston harbor, a British revenue cutter rides at anchor off America's first lighthouse, built in 1716. The lantern atop its 75-foot stone tower blazed from sunset to sunrise and consumed five tons of whale oil a year. During periods of heavy fog, when the light could not be seen from a distance, the cannon near the base of the lighthouse was fired at frequent intervals.

have astonished the Puritans of the previous century, he paraded his wealth at every opportunity. He purchased land on prestigious Beacon Hill and built a brick mansion that was the envy of all Boston. Glass windows were a sign of great prosperity in those days, and the Hancock house had 54 of them. Those on the south face of the house overlooked a series of gardens landscaped in spare-no-expense style. "It's allowed on all hands," Hancock wrote when sending for a shipment of plants from a London horticulturist, "the Kingdom of England don't afford so fine a prospect as I have." The sights inside his house were equally pleasant to behold; they included such luxuries as wallpaper that Hancock had ordered from England, asking that it be "extraordinarily neat and the figures and colors beautiful," and a chiming clock that had, by his account, "three handsome carved figures, gilt with burnished gold."

Hancock adorned himself as lavishly as the house. In 1756 he wrote to one of his agents in London: "I want a very handsome sword for myself. Let it be a fashionable one, whether a neat silver-washed or one most in taste that gentlemen wear." In a portrait of him at leisure in the privacy of his home, he is shown attired in a blue damask dressing gown, a white satin waistcoat, black satin breeches, a red velvet cap, red morocco slippers and white silk stockings. In another portrait of him in his counting-house garb, he wears a blue broadcloth coat with gold lacing and long lace ruffles at the wrists, a tricornered hat set on a powdered wig tied in a queue, and shoes with silver buckles.

To get about the city, he ordered from England a conveyance that he described as a "covered chariot," giving as a reason for the purchase the intelligence that "Mrs. Hancock is often ill, and we live so far from town and church that an open chaise is very inconvenient for her." Hancock went on to specify that "it be a new, neat, and very good one," adding: "Let everything be of the best and fashionable." As a final elegant touch, he requested that a coachman be sent from London, one who was known to be "sober, and honest and one that understands a kitchen garden, to keep from being idle, not younger than twenty-six or twenty-eight nor older than thirty to thirty-six."

In some 40 years of vigorous and imaginative enterprise, Hancock amassed a fortune of almost £100,000. He was among the richest men in all the colonies, although by midcentury at least 20 other New England merchants were worth about £80,000. There is no doubt that, as with Hancock, a great deal of their wealth was acquired by evasion of the laws of trade. For all that, many colonists still thought of England as the home country and of themselves as Englishmen—and none more so than Thomas Hancock. Despite a lifetime devoted to figuring ways to beat the Crown to profits he thought himself entitled to, he contemplated retiring to England to live out his last days. But he never acted on this sentiment. On August 1, 1764, as he was entering the Massachusetts State House, where he served as a councilman, he was stricken with apoplexy. Two hours later he was dead.

Control of the business passed to his adopted nephew John, and another era began. John represented a new generation of colonists—one that, instead of evading the English authorities, would confront them.

Thomas Hancock, a Boston merchant, amassed one of America's greatest fortunes during the first half of the 18th Century by systematically flouting British trade regulations. His vessels left Boston with legitimate cargoes of rum, whale oil and fish; on the return trip, they off-loaded contraband consignments of tea, wine and molasses outside the harbor, then—all innocence—sailed into port to undergo customs inspection.

The stakes were higher than ever. Twenty per cent of all shipping traffic to Britain came from the American colonies, and the tobacco, timber, whale oil, rum and other goods brought in on these vessels were valued at £1.3 million—up from £400,000 at the turn of the century. Many of England's industrial towns were engaged in producing cutlery, haberdashery, tools, blankets and other goods for colonial markets. These exported English manufactures, together with such commodities transshipped from elsewhere in Europe, totaled £2.5 million—up from £350,000 in 1700. The colonial trade had become a cornerstone of the British economy.

Four years before John Hancock inherited his uncle's business, a very determined young man had acceded to the throne of England as King George III. He intended to go down in history as a great leader, and one way he set about realizing that ambition was to crack down hard on the colonists. At his behest, Parliament began enacting new duties on such luxury items as wine and silk. George III took steps to improve the performance of the customs service: He insisted on all manner of documentation to show where merchantmen obtained their cargoes, and he ordained that smugglers henceforth would be tried in London-controlled Admiralty courts, which had neither juries nor any colonial representation.

There was to be nothing lackadaisical about enforcement of his mercantile policies. English men-of-war that had been employed in a recent war against the French were now sent to the American coast to be used against smugglers. In an even harsher move, George III sanctioned English privateers to prey upon American vessels that dared to trade with the French or the Dutch. Together, those two actions had repercussions that George III and his advisers found unsettling. Previously, the various colonies had tended to go their own separate ways in political matters. Now they came to see that they had a common adversary. "An attack made on one of our sister Colonies, to compel submission to arbitrary taxes, is an attack made on all British America," said Governor John Dunmore of Virginia.

Few men in America were more visibly committed to this view of colonial rights than John Hancock. Willowy, aristocratic-looking and only 27 years old when he came into his inheritance, he must have seemed an unlikely revolutionary. Since his graduation from Harvard in 1754 he had worked in the Hancock countinghouse in Boston and done one stint abroad to learn about foreign markets. Another eminent New Englander, John Adams, described him as a paragon of diligence in those early years: "Wholly devoted to business, he was regular and punctual at his store as the sun in his course." He was also a society figure and—even more than his uncle—a leader of fashion. His penchant for a scarlet coat was widely noted, and he sometimes wore jackets and breeches that were lilac-colored.

His first concern was to expand the operations of the House of Hancock. He commissioned more oceangoing ships, and fancied them up as he did his own person, ordering them decorated in various shades of blue, red, yellow and green. He also purchased additional whaling vessels in order to take advantage of the expansion of the whale-oil market.

John Hancock, nephew and heir of Thomas Hancock, thundered against the restrictions that the Crown placed on colonial merchants. When he signed the Declaration of Independence in 1776, he made a point of scrawling his name large enough "so George III may read without his spectacles."

The October 31, 1765, issue of The
Pennsylvania Journal carries a lugubrious
farewell from its owner, announcing
that he would suspend publication rather
than comply with the onerous Stamp Act
of 1765. The Act produced so many
retaliatory threats by American merchants
that it was swiftly repealed—and The
Pennsylvania Journal stayed in business.

In two years' time, he managed to increase the sales of the House of
Hancock by more than 50 per cent.

But John Hancock's real mission in life was politics. From the time
he took control of the firm, he sought to win influence in colonial affairs.
In 1765 he ran for the General Court of Massachusetts, but he came in last
with only 40 votes. By way of improving on this showing, he later held
what a contemporary described as a "grand and elegant entertainment to
the genteel part of the town, and treated the populace with a pipe of
Madeira wine." The extravaganza, which included a dazzling display of
fireworks, repaid him handsomely; when Hancock ran again for the
General Court six months later, he was elected by a substantial margin.

He also began to take a stance against British repression. When word
reached the colonies in 1765 that Parliament had passed the Stamp Act,
requiring the purchase of stamps that had to be affixed to commercial
and legal papers and publications, Hancock castigated the legislation as
a "great burthen laid upon us." In protest, he withdrew his ships from
service with England. Many other merchants did the same.

But the Stamp Act, with its tax on such commonplace items as newspapers and almanacs, pinched more than the big merchants. Disaffection spread through a broad segment of colonial society. Groups calling themselves the Sons of Liberty sprang up in Boston, New York and Philadelphia, and threatened violent action against anyone who upheld the British tax measure. In Boston, a mob destroyed the office of the chief stamp collector, attacked the homes of customs men and burned the records of the Admiralty court. In New York, the Sons of Liberty threw bricks at British soldiers, set the Lieutenant Governor's coach ablaze, gutted a British official's house and then burned its furnishings in the street. In Philadelphia, mobs destroyed large quantities of the stamps.

The riots went unheeded in England, but after English merchants began to feel the withdrawal of colonial ships from their harbors that year, Parliament was induced to repeal the Stamp Act. For the first time, the colonists had won a concession from the mother country.

Hancock himself was soon provoked into a deed that made him a hero to the Massachusetts patriots. In April of 1768, customs officials boarded one of his ships, the *Lydia*, as she lay in the harbor; they suspected that she was concealing an illegal cargo. Hancock was outraged and sped to the scene with a pair of henchmen, who dragged the customs men up from the hold and forcibly removed them from the ship before they could investigate the contents. The authorities decided that, since they had no firm evidence of smuggling, they could not prosecute. But the deed had wide and lasting implications: It inspired more such overt refusals to comply with the demands of the British officials.

A month later, another Hancock ship, the *Liberty*, arrived from Madeira with a cargo of wine. Shortly afterward, a 50-gun British man-of-war, the *Romney*, put into Boston harbor. The local customs commissioners, acting on a tip that more wine had been unloaded from Hancock's ship than had been declared on the lading list, seized the *Liberty* with the help of the *Romney*'s crew and proceeded to tow her away. Meanwhile, a crowd had gathered at dockside; some men grabbed the *Liberty*'s ropes to hold her back, and others threw stones at the *Romney*'s men. The customs officials, giving up their mission, turned to go home; the mob followed, stoning them and smashing the windows of their houses.

The furor over that incident had no sooner died down than Parliament passed another set of repressive acts. These measures, called the Townshend Acts for the member of Parliament who had sponsored them, imposed taxes on such basic items as tea, glass and paper. Inevitably, the Acts provoked further mob action. British officials, customs collectors, and colonists who informed on smugglers were beaten and tarred and feathered. Groups of unruly protesters assembled at the slightest provocation. To try to maintain some order, the Crown installed detachments of red-coated British soldiers in Boston and in New York. In 1770 a mob taunted a group of the soldiers stationed in Boston; the soldiers opened fire, five colonists were killed, and the patriots had a cause célèbre—the Boston Massacre. "Boston people are run mad," reported the newly appointed royal Governor.

Against this background, Hancock's shipping business languished, but his political career flourished. He was already active as a Boston

selectman and as a member of the Massachusetts General Court. After the Boston Massacre, he became chairman of a committee created expressly for the purpose of demanding removal of the British troops. The committee protested in vain; the troops stayed on.

Boston, as the busiest port, was the focus of most colonial discontent. But other ports were not exempt from British surveillance, and they shared in the Bostonians' sense of affront. The year before the Boston Massacre took place, citizens of Newport took memorable action against the British customs service. Their specific target was an armed revenue cutter that—like one of Hancock's ships, but rather less aptly—bore the name *Liberty*. This sloop, captained by a particularly zealous customs man, seized an American brig in Long Island Sound on July 17, 1769, and took the vessel into Newport. The captain of the brig, a man named Packwood, was able to show that his cargo was entirely legal. Nonetheless, he was detained by the authorities for several days and given no indication of when his case would be dealt with. The exasperated Packwood finally went aboard the revenue cutter and demanded that his brig be allowed to continue on her way. At this point, relates a chronicler of the episode, "some difficulty took place between Packwood and the men

The revenue cutter Gaspée *burns in Narragansett Bay in 1772, having been set afire by eight boatloads of Rhode Islanders in retaliation for her zealous inspection of American vessels.*

in the *Liberty* which resulted in several musket shots being fired at Packwood's boat as it was returning shoreward."

The men of Newport had had enough. They went aboard the *Liberty* and cut her adrift. When she fetched up on the shore, they chopped down her masts and tossed all of her guns into the harbor. A short while later, the tide lifted the British sloop off the shore. She drifted to a nearby island and there was subjected to a final, fatal expression of colonial wrath. During the night, a group of patriots visited the island and set the hapless *Liberty* ablaze.

A similar event took place outside Providence one night in 1772, when the British warship *Gaspée* ran aground on a sandspit while chasing a sloop suspected of smuggling. Noting the *Gaspée*'s vulnerability, a group of local merchants met in a tavern and planned a vicious blow against British oppression. One of them offered the use of eight boats. The men armed themselves and, with muffled oars, silently rowed out to the sandspit. They shot and badly wounded the *Gaspée*'s commander, and captured the crew and removed them from the ship. The attackers then set the *Gaspée* on fire and gleefully watched her burn. When the British authorities questioned local people about the incident, no one admitted to even an awareness of the deed.

In the following year, passions reached a pitch that clouded reason. Parliament went to the aid of the financially troubled British East India Company, allowing it to pay lower duties on tea than colonial merchants were required to pay. Since this threatened to force the American shippers out of the trade altogether, they boycotted the cheaper tea. Shipments were locked away in warehouses, and many tea ships were prevented from entering colonial ports at all. In Boston, colonists refused to unload the cargoes of three tea ships, and they urged the royal Governor to issue clearance papers that would send the ships back to England. But the Governor—whose two sons and nephew happened to have a financial interest in the cargo—refused to grant the colonists' request. He ordered that the duty be paid on the unloaded tea within 20 days.

As the days passed, news of the dispute spread out from Boston. On the morning of December 16, 1773, the 20th day, people started pouring into the city to see what would happen when the grace period expired. By nightfall some 8,000 had assembled—yet the Governor had taken no action, and still the ships lay in the harbor. The mob, now aroused to fever pitch, took matters into their own hands. Some of them, disguised as Indians, boarded the ships and dumped the contents of 342 chests of tea into the bay. Soon colonists up and down the coast learned of the episode, and they expressed their approval in violent demonstrations against the British authorities.

A few months later, the tea issue spawned another orgy of destruction, this time in Annapolis. The victims were Americans—shipowning merchants who, in spite of public objections, had brought in a cargo of tea on a vessel called the *Peggy Stewart*. These businessmen were already unpopular in the community, having more than once imported British goods that the public wanted kept out. When they now made haste to pay the necessary tax so that the tea could be put up for sale, a group of Maryland citizens assembled and discussed retaliatory steps. Throwing

In a cartoon published in London in 1774, sadistic-looking Bostonians pour tea down the throat of a tarred-and-feathered customs officer charged with enforcing the Tea Act; the Act was designed to give London merchants a monopoly on the tea trade. Tea was a staple beverage in America and a major source of revenue for the colonists—until the hated act took effect.

The BOSTONIAN'S Paying the EXCISE-MAN, or TARRING & FEATHERING the tea into the harbor was proposed, but many of those present at the meeting rejected such a measure as too mild a punishment. One man suggested that the tea be unloaded and then pointedly burned under the town gallows. Other participants insisted that the offending merchants should lose their ship—and this extreme remedy was the one chosen in the end. Before a great crowd, the *Peggy Stewart* was set ablaze in the Annapolis harbor with all her sails set, and she went to the bottom with the tea. As a final penalty, her owners had to make a written apology for their "most daring insult."

The British reacted to such incidents with fury. They passed a series of laws certain to further alienate the colonists. Debate and elections were curtailed. And henceforth, no colonist would be permitted to hold office without royal approval.

These acts—which came to be known in America as the Coercive Acts—finally tipped the balance, provoking the colonists into concerted action to win the rights they believed should be theirs. In the fall of 1774 the First Continental Congress assembled in Philadelphia and voted to cut off all trade with England unless the Coercive Acts were repealed. Instead, Parliament struck back with yet another round of laws, prohibiting New England from trading with any part of the world except Great Britain and Ireland and refusing colonial fishermen access to the fishing banks of Newfoundland.

Now the flash point had been reached. Smuggling had failed to get around the English, and Parliamentary acts had failed to subdue the colonists. The next step, inevitably, was open combat. On the night of April 18, 1775, British troops moved out from Boston to destroy supplies of arms and ammunition in Concord, and the war was on.

Eight years of fighting followed. The real thrust of American activity was in privateering at sea. The Continental Congress issued 626 letters of marque to Massachusetts vessels alone, and about 1,000 more authorizations were issued by the General Court of Massachusetts. Some 20,000 Americans sailed on privateers, 2,000 more than fought in George Washington's Continental Army. Operating all over the Atlantic, from the American coast to the English Channel—and even into the North Sea—they captured some 800 British vessels; Salem privateers alone captured more than 445.

Many of the prizes were military vessels. In June of 1776, three American privateers attacked two heavily armed British transports off Nantasket Roads, Massachusetts; after some stiff fighting at close quarters, the British gave up, and 200 British soldiers were captured. In a particularly heroic action, a single letter-of-marque ship, the 14-gun *General Pickering* of Salem, defeated a British warship three times her size, despite being handicapped by a full cargo of sugar.

The heroics were more than matched by profits. An early prize was the British brigantine *Nancy*, taken off Cape Ann, Massachusetts, in November 1775 by the 72-ton schooner *Lee*. The value of the ship and her cargo was more than £20,000. Of that, £6,574 was divided among the *Lee's* captain, John Manley, and his crew. (Along with about 60 other captains of privateers, Manley went on to become a captain in the American Navy, which was formed during the last years of the war.)

Shipowners received the greatest share of the privateering profits, and over the full course of the Revolutionary War a few of them built immense fortunes this way; Robert Morris, a Philadelphian, was said to have made eight million dollars. English shipping fortunes were, of course, correspondingly depleted. It was partly because of pressure from London merchants, alarmed at their losses, that England finally surrendered on October 19, 1781.

With independence a reality, the American merchants were able to operate completely in the open for the first time. Congress authorized commercial agreements with France, Spain, the Netherlands, Prussia, Sweden and Russia. The new American Minister to France—Virginia planter Thomas Jefferson—went to Paris and made arrangements for tobacco and rice to be shipped to France. And after a brief cooling-off period, the tobacco merchants began dealing with England again: England had nowhere else to turn for the now-indispensable imports of tobacco, rice, indigo and naval stores, and was glad enough to resume relations with its rebellious offspring. By 1786, three years after the peace had been signed, tobacco exports to England totaled 51,000 pounds—more than they had been before the war.

New England did not recover as quickly as the agricultural South, because much of its wealth had been invested in the shipping industry. The fishing and whaling fleets of the Northern colonies had been destroyed during the war. Now, even with the hostilities ended, England forbade the British West Indies from trading with the new nation and showed no willingness to buy ships built in New England.

But Massachusetts merchants had their own need for ships. Furthermore, they had no difficulty in developing new patterns of trade. They headed for the Baltic, shipping rum from their own distilleries, flour that they had picked up in Philadelphia, and tobacco that they had loaded in Chesapeake Bay; in exchange, they obtained iron from Sweden and sailcloth and cordage from Russia. Then the West Indies opened up. The sugar-producing islands still had no basic food crops, and so officials there were glad enough to look the other way when American vessels sailed in with fish, meat and flour. And by 1787 England had reopened trading with New Englanders. (John Hancock was not among the beneficiaries; he had given up a merchant's career to serve as Governor of Massachusetts.) By the start of the next decade, England was once again the principal trading partner of merchants in the North as well as the South.

Despite the nit-picking of Randolph, despite the threats of enforcement of the Navigation Acts at gunpoint, despite the constant danger of attack by pirates or privateers looking for loot and despite the natural hazards of the stormy crossing, the transatlantic trade had never for any length of time ceased growing. But now, in the years that followed the war, the tempo of activity on the North Atlantic was to become faster by far. Emigration continued to accelerate. The Industrial Revolution was under way on both sides of the ocean, lending a new dynamism to the economies of the transatlantic trading partners. At the same time, the economy of the American South changed in a way that fit England's

needs perfectly: Cotton production began to overtake tobacco production. During the four-year period from 1791 to 1795, the plantations of the South produced 5.2 million pounds of cotton. In the middle of that period—1793—the cotton gin was invented, and cotton output began to shoot upward; the yield during the next four years was 18.2 million pounds.

For the time being, shipping practices lagged behind the advances ashore. Ships sailed when the weather was fair and at the captain's pleasure. Communications remained primitive. People generally had to take the precaution of sending several copies of letters by different vessels to make certain that at least one copy got through. Merchants often operated in the dark, buying goods without knowing the state of the markets in the countries where they would sell them. There was still no direct, official mail service between the Old World and the New: Since 1755 the British government had been running 200-ton brigs that specialized in carrying mail across the Atlantic, but these ships traveled by way of Nova Scotia in the summer and Bermuda in the winter.

Merchantmen sailing directly across the Atlantic could deliver the mail faster, and most international communications were simply left in port coffeehouses to be picked up by the master of a vessel bound for Europe or America. Still, an exchange of letters across the ocean often took half a year or longer.

The armed schooner Lee, *one of some 2,000 American privateers that preyed on British shipping during the Revolution, leads the munitions ship* Nancy *into Gloucester, Massachusetts, in 1775. The* Nancy's *cargo included 2,000 muskets, 31 tons of musket shot, 3,000 cannon shot and several barrels of gunpowder.*

*Five American privateers engage in
a running fight with the armed transports
Annabella and Howe off the coast of
Massachusetts on the 17th of June, 1776.
The transports, carrying 210 Scottish
Highlanders, were among 33 troop carriers
that had sailed from Scotland for Boston.
Colonial vessels captured eight of them.*

To Thomas Jefferson, waiting in Paris in the summer of 1785 for instructions from his government, such a state of affairs was exasperating. He therefore wrote a modest proposal:

> To send a packet from each port once in two months, the business might possibly be done by two packets, as will be seen by the following scheme, wherein we will call the two packets A. and B.
>
> Jan. A. sails from New York, B. from Havre.
> Feb.
> March. B. New York. A. Havre.
> Apr.
> May. A. New York. B. Havre.
> June.
> July. B. New York. A. Havre. . . .

As it turned out, Jefferson was 34 years ahead of his time, and when a direct packet service was finally inaugurated, it would be with England, not France. But he saw the future clearly. A momentous development in transatlantic travel and transport was coming, and it would make the North Atlantic the busiest of the world's ocean highways. Moreover, this development was as breathtakingly simple as the past was turmoiled: Ships would sail to timetables.

The seaboard conduits
of American trade

"No nation in the world possesses vaster, deeper or more secure ports for commerce than the Americas," wrote the French chronicler Alexis de Tocqueville after traveling through the United States in the early 19th Century.

He might have added that no nation had built up its seaports so rapidly or so effectively. After the winning of independence and the permanent removal of English taxes and embargoes in 1781, the ports on the Atlantic seaboard swelled from small trading marts to intricate mazes of wharves, warehouses, countinghouses and other facilities in service of commerce.

In 1819, Boston erected a semaphore tower on a hill eight miles outside the city to signal the arrival of oceangoing vessels at the entrance to Massachusetts Bay; the messages were then picked up by a watchman who was stationed in another tower built on the wharves. In the meantime New Yorkers, as author James Fenimore Cooper reported to a European friend, were "daily constructing great ranges of wooden piers in order to meet the increasing demands of trade." Eventually, New York's piers would occupy seven miles of waterfront.

Ports had, of course, been essential to American prosperity from the start; William Penn chose the site of Philadelphia for his "great towne" only after sounding the Delaware River for some 30 miles in search of the most convenient harbor for the 300-ton ocean vessels of his day. Charleston was founded in 1670 because English merchants wanted a trading post on the mainland to supply their colonies in the West Indies—and Charleston was as far south as they could settle without meeting resistance from Spain.

Even as settlement pushed westward across the Appalachians during the 18th Century, the ports remained the financial and cultural centers of the young nation, and the greatest centers of population. No inland city would exceed the size of any of the five major ports shown here and on the following pages until 1870, when Chicago's population surpassed that of Boston. To the men and women making their way across the Atlantic, America's ports were nothing less than marvels of concentrated energy. An Englishman debarking in New York early in the 19th Century remarked, "Every thought, word, look and action of the multitude seemed to be absorbed by commerce."

A three-masted warship and hundreds of oceangoing trading vessels line New York harbor, just beyond the stone walls of a fort on Governor's Island. In the early 19th Century, when this engraving was made, New York's wharves were no more than a long framework filled with loose stones and then surfaced with trodden earth. Some of the slips that were formed by these wharves could admit as many as 30 or 40 sail at a time.

In Boston harbor, watermen in dinghies hover about a topsail schooner, a barge and a raft of sawed timbers. At the time of the nation's birth, Boston possessed marine facilities unequaled by any other American port. "Vessels may unship their cargoes at the very doors of bordering warehouses," commented an admiring visitor from New York. The waterfront windmill was one of three such structures in the city—employed for grinding grain, driving saws and pumping water.

Under the spreading elm on the Delaware River where William Penn signed a treaty with the Indians and founded Philadelphia in 1682. Nineteenth Century shipwrights work on some small vessels. By the year 1800, shipbuilding was one of Philadelphia's major industries and an important factor in coastal trade; 90 per cent of the shipwrights' wood was imported from elsewhere in the nation—mulberry from Maryland and Virginia, live oak and red cedar from North and South Carolina and Georgia.

A lone steersman guides a grain barge past a flotilla of ocean, coastal and river packets crowding New Orleans harbor. The acquisition of Louisiana in 1803 provided a lucrative entrepôt for the yield of the hinterland; during the five-year period ending in 1821, more than $16 million worth of cotton and other goods traveled down the Mississippi River for export from New Orleans. Cargo awaiting transshipment was stored in the open on earthen levees until 1836, when the first warehouse was built.

On a marshy bank opposite the wharves of Mobile, Alabama, two watermen calk the bottom of a skiff while other workers apply planks to a sloop they are building. Situated 40 miles from the Gulf of Mexico at the junction of the Mobile and Tensaw Rivers, the port specialized in transshipping cotton brought from inland plantations by riverboat. More than 13 million 500-pound bales were loaded on outbound vessels between 1817 and 1860. Most of the cotton went to Britain and France.

Against a backdrop of thunderclouds and a rainbow, river and oceangoing vessels vie for anchorage in Charleston harbor, at the confluence of the Ashley and Cooper Rivers. As the only one of the southern ports with direct access to the Atlantic Ocean, Charleston was the commercial center for a 700-mile-long coastal area that extended from southern Virginia to Spanish Florida. The city grew rich on exports of rice, cotton and indigo, an important source of 19th Century fabric dye.

Chapter 3
A scheduling revolution

anuary 5, 1818, dawned bitterly cold in New York City, and a biting northeast wind sent gusts of snow swirling about the waterfront along South Street. It was no day to expect a transatlantic sailing. But at one pier, seamen clambered in the rigging of the 424-ton merchantman *James Monroe*, wiping away the gathering snow with their bare hands, setting canvas and hoisting a flag emblazoned with a black ball on a red field. Longshoremen lumbered aboard with 1,500 barrels of apples, 860 barrels of flour, 200 barrels of potash, 71 bales of cotton, 14 bales of wool, coops of hens, a few cows, pigs and sheep on the hoof, and a rawhide bag full of mail. As the morning wore on, eight passengers strode up the gangplank.

When the bells of St. Paul's Church chimed 10 o'clock, Captain James Watkinson gave the order to cast off. The seamen sheeted in the sails, and the *James Monroe* swung into the bay—to a rousing cheer from a group of waterfront bystanders, who had watched the proceedings with curiosity and not a little skepticism. The *James Monroe* was bound for Liverpool, sailing as promised, despite the January storm and the fact that her hold had room for another 1,000 barrels of cargo and her cabins room for another 20 passengers.

Never before in memory had ship merchants dared to promise delivery of transatlantic cargoes by prearranged schedule; they and the captains of their ships normally waited for full holds, for an extra passenger or two, and for clear skies and fair winds before setting sail. The prompt departure of the *James Monroe* heralded a bold—even revolutionary—business venture.

The new enterprise had been organized 10 weeks before by Isaac Wright, a New York merchant, in collaboration with four partners and a number of Liverpool connections. Three of the partners—Benjamin Marshall, and the brothers Jeremiah and Francis Thompson—were Englishmen who had taken up residence in New York to handle the imports of their family woolen textile business. The other—Isaac Wright's son William—lived on Long Island and, together with his father, exported cotton for weaving in England. All had long been impatient with the dilatory sailings that then prevailed.

Each of the men put up about $25,000 to finance a little fleet of four ships. And, on the 27th of October, they placed an eye-catching advertisement in the New York *Evening Post*. "In order to furnish

Her fore-topsail bearing the insignia of the Red Star Line of New York, the 616-ton packet Virginian courses the open sea. Within three decades of the founding of the first packet line in 1818, more than 50 such ships plied the Atlantic on regular schedules, and the port of New York alone averaged three arrivals and three departures per week.

frequent and regular conveyances for GOODS and PASSENGERS," they wrote, they had "undertaken to establish a line of vessels between NEW YORK and LIVERPOOL, to sail from each place on a certain day in every month throughout the year." A corresponding notice published in Liverpool promised "a regular succession of Vessels, which will *positively sail, full or not full.*"

In pledging to make regular sailings of their four ships, Wright and his partners were taking a considerable gamble. There was always the possibility that the ships might have to make the crossings without sufficient cargo and passengers to cover costs. The vessels were also likely to suffer unusual wear and tear, as they would be tackling the Atlantic in all seasons. One captain who battled through a winter gale remembered: "After a course of protracted flapping in that violent wind, many pieces of the torn sails became so knotted and braided that a marline-spike could not penetrate them."

But offsetting the risks was the opportunity to reap splendid profits. In the lusty rebirth of commerce that followed the War for Independence and its postscript, the War of 1812, the mills of England demanded cotton in record quantities. The plantations of the American South answered the call with bounteous yields; 156,000 bales of cotton would leave the port of New Orleans in 1822. And, in time, the developing western hinterland added such foodstuffs as flour and cheese as exports. Of the latter commodity, an English visitor to the New York waterfront was to write in 1843 that every ship "takes out immense quantities of this article. Who would ever have thought of John Bull eating Yankee cheese? It sells in England at forty to fifty cents a hundred pounds, which pays freight and charges, and leaves Brother Jonathan"—contemporary British slang for Americans—"a pretty good profit." Another lucrative cargo was specie, or coined money, which constantly crossed the Atlantic in both directions because many shipping transactions were made in cash.

The port of New York was a hive of maritime activity by the time Isaac Wright and his partners set up their Atlantic shuttle. Bales, barrels, hogsheads, chests and casks of various commodities crowded the waterfront. Drays and wheelbarrows, horses and pedestrians all jostled for right of way. "Everything was in motion," reported one impressed visitor from abroad. At the intersection of Wall and Water Streets, a block or two from the waterfront, auctioneers stood on the steps of the Tontine Coffee House—a favorite gathering place of businessmen—taking bids from buyers who shouted from the street. Inside the coffeehouse, brokers and underwriters negotiated shipping contracts and insured cargoes. Repairing to their countinghouses, the owners carried on correspondence with merchants at home and abroad, made the final judgment on when it was time to overhaul a vessel, decided which captains were appropriate for assignment to which ships. And if they had nothing more pressing to do, they served as salesmen on the waterfront, ushering prospective passengers aboard their ships and explaining to them why no other conveyance would do.

Practically all of New York's shipping merchants lived within walking distance of their countinghouses and within sight of the ships pass-

Horse carts, barrels, bales and lumber crowd the street in front of the Tontine Coffee House (left), where New York merchants and shipowners would meet to swap financial gossip and arrange business ventures over a good meal.

ing up and down the East River. The shipowners got up so early in the morning that they came to be known, half-jokingly, half-admiringly, as Peep O' Day Boys. By 5:30 a.m. some of them were already strolling along the waterfront, checking out the vessels in port, inspecting cargo on the docks, conferring with their colleagues at the Merchants' Exchange. When word reached the countinghouse that a ship had entered New York harbor, the owner would call out "Boy, give me a spy glass!" and race to the window to see if the vessel was his. If it was, he would hire a boatman to scull him out to meet the vessel. Then he personally supervised the unloading of the ship's cargo, often directing his own crews of longshoremen and stevedores.

Workdays typically ended late. Most merchants belonged to a club called the House of Lords, sponsored by the Baker City Tavern at 4 Wall Street. Every weekday night at 7:30, the membership convened. Each man was allowed a limited amount of liquor and not a drop more, for business was the object—and it was discussed until 10 o'clock, when the House of Lords adjourned.

Wright and his partners anticipated that in this humming market, merchants with cargoes to send, officials with important missions to execute and anyone with a missive to post would be willing to pay premium rates for guaranteed service.

Ships await passengers and cargo at piers along New York's South Street, aptly known as Packet Row. Novelist Charles Dickens visited the spot in 1842 and wrote in amazement that bowsprits "almost thrust themselves into the windows" across the way.

They were proved right. By the end of the first year, the new line's four packets had each made three round trips between New York and Liverpool—sometimes without full holds, but always on schedule unless they had been delayed by truly dreadful weather. Concern with schedule naturally gave rise to an interest in speed, and the ships completed their passages in record-breaking times. By piling on sail day and night, they reduced the eastward, so-called downhill, passage (which ran with the prevailing westerlies and the eastward-flowing Gulf Stream) from a month or so to an average of 24 days, and they trimmed the westward, or uphill, crossing from about three months to an average of 40 days.

So successful was the Black Ball Line—as it came to be known, after the emblem on the house flag—that it soon attracted competition. The year 1822 saw the founding of two more lines operating between New York and Liverpool—the Red Star and the Swallowtail, each with four ships. At the same time, the Black Ball's fleet expanded to eight ships, bringing the total number of New York-to-Liverpool ships to 16—and making the sailings weekly occurrences. These vessels and others like them clearly deserved a name of their own, and the public gave them one: The term "packet"—heretofore applied indiscriminately to miscellaneous vessels that carried cargoes bundled in packets— came to signify a ship that sailed on schedule, and hence a ship that could be counted on to deliver the most urgent cargoes, important mail and time-pressed passengers of the day.

For another half century—until steam, with its special boons and special hazards, brought a new dimension to seaborne travel—sailing ships of the sort assembled by Isaac Wright and his partners became the major vehicles of transatlantic communication, heirs to the doughty colonizing vessels that had established the Atlantic connection in the first place and to the succeeding array of merchantmen that had turned the ocean into a highway during the 18th Century. By the year 1843, as many as 24 packets plied the route between New York and Liverpool alone, and a number of others sailed eastward from Boston, Philadelphia and Baltimore, and westward from London, Le Havre and Antwerp. All these were supplemented by a network of coastal packet lines running between New York and Charleston, Savannah, New Orleans and Mobile. They also connected with river packets plying the Hudson, the Mississippi and other waterways into the continent, and ultimately they drew on a canal system hundreds of miles in extent.

The ocean-spanning shuttles were, of course, the key to the whole maritime system. That they succeeded so well was not only a testament to the vision of shipowners like Isaac Wright, but also a reflection of the consummate skills of packet captains, the hardihood of the crewmen—and the marvelous efficacy of the ships themselves.

Aside from the bold symbols that dominated their house flags and their fore-topsails—the black ball, the red star, the blue swallowtail on the three initial lines, and comparable symbols on subsequent ones—there was little to distinguish the early packets from the ordinary merchantmen of the day. Every packet was a square-rigger with three masts—fore,

Quick to capitalize on a good idea, shipowner Thomas P. Cope adopted New York's packet-line concept for his hometown of Philadelphia in 1822. His firm of Cope & Son, offering direct sailings between Philadelphia and Liverpool every month, continued in operation for nearly four decades.

A poster for the firm of Train & Company advertises the entry of Boston into the packet trade. The firm, which was established in 1844 as the tide of immigration began to rise, eventually had 30 ships flying its White Diamond flag and earned one million dollars a year.

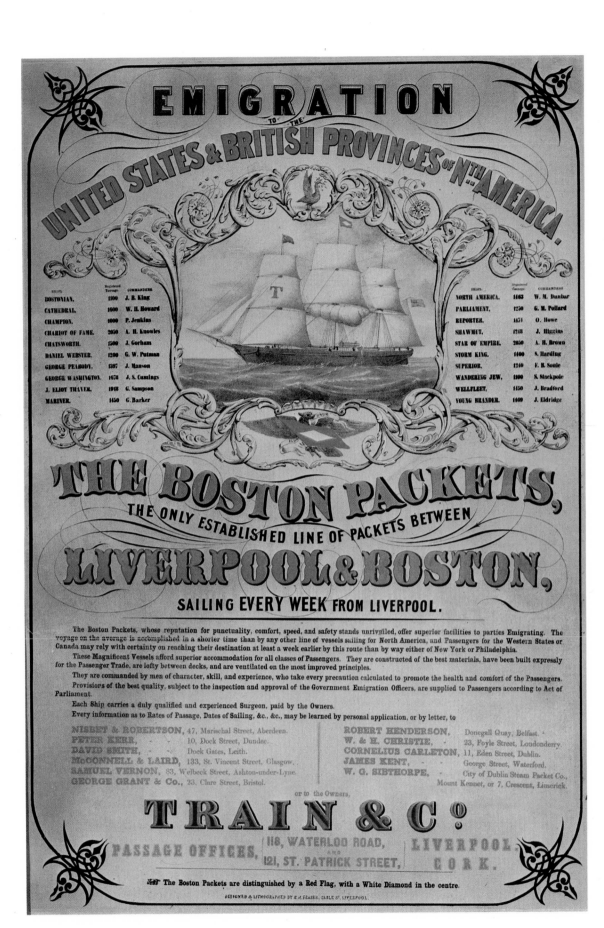

main and mizzen. And every packet was built to carry all the canvas it could—and then some. Each mast came in three pieces: the thick lower mast, which extended down to the keelson; the topmast, above the lower mast and slightly overlapping it; and above the topmast, the slender topgallant mast. The mainmast carried, from bottom to top, a mainsail, a main-topsail, a main-topgallant sail and a main royal. The foremast carried similar canvas. On the mizzenmast the lower sail, or spanker, ran aft from the mast instead of being square-rigged, and at the bow, the bowsprit extended as a boom to support jib sails.

The packets were all tubby in appearance—blunt of bow, rounded on the sides and V-bottomed. The Black Ball Line's *James Monroe*, which had already completed seven months' service before her pioneering run on schedule, was more or less typical; she was 118 feet in length and a bit more than 28 feet in the beam—or roughly four times as long as she was wide. Her hold was a commodious 14 feet in depth, spacious enough to stow more than 3,500 barrels of cargo.

By the middle of the 1830s, shipyards along the New York waterfront were building expressly for the packet trade—and for the functions that the packet had to fulfill. First and foremost, the packet served as a cargo carrier, and as volume increased, the size of the ships themselves grew from an average of 400 tons to 500 tons, then 800 tons; eventually, in the 1850s, the packets would peak at 1,700 tons. As the ships became larger, their bottoms became flatter—in part because it was discovered that the flat-bottomed hulls built to negotiate the sandbars at the mouth of the Mississippi River could run through the water as fast as any vessels afloat, and also because flat bottoms provided more cargo space and greater stability, qualities that were crucial to the merchants engaged in the transatlantic trade. The only drawback was that the packet butted into the waves instead of cutting them, a trait little appreciated by passengers.

From the beginning, passenger traffic was important, and the packets tried to entice travelers aboard with promises of comfort and style. This provoked some journalistic mirth at the *New York Herald*. "What next?" asked one of its reporters on seeing the packet *Liverpool* and finding that her main saloon "is large enough for forty cabin passengers and is high enough for any man under eight feet in his boots." But comfort became a small consideration (to the owners at least) when emigration from the British Isles swelled in the 1850s; most of the packets' westbound revenue then came from emigrants who were desperate to reach America but too poor and too needy to be choosy about how they got there. The packets crammed hundreds of men, women and children into steerage, the upper hold between the decks, which was used for cargo on the eastbound passage.

Sturdy construction was a requirement for every packet, no matter what its size or role, for there was no more demanding career for a ship than year-round service on the Atlantic. Owners—and captains, who took increasingly active roles in supervising design and construction—ordered the packets built of costly cedar, locust and live oak; in the 1830s, owners were paying anywhere from $40,000 to $50,000 per ship. That was a substantial investment, but one with a high re-

Backing her main-topsail and hauling aboard her port boat, the 573-ton packet Orpheus sets out on a voyage from New York to Liverpool in 1835. The Orpheus was one of nine vessels then sailing under the Black Ball flag.

turn. A packet carrying full cargoes might earn as much as $20,000 on freight in a year, and an additional $10,000 from passengers, specie and mail. Even allowing for maintenance costs, the vessel could pay for herself in two or three years.

With their combined assets of regularity, speed and ruggedness, the packets won universal admiration. Two lines of a seaman's ditty ran: "With every stitch drawing aloft and alow / She's a Liverpool packet, Lord God, see her go!" Charles Dickens, who sailed in one in 1842, offered a more explicit assessment. "The noble American vessels," he wrote, "have made their packet service the finest in the world."

The men who crewed the packet ships came largely from the coasts of New England, where they began going out on fishing expeditions in boyhood. Wherever they came from, they were a special breed. "Aboard of those liners," wrote novelist Herman Melville, who went to sea as a ship's boy in 1839, "the crew have terrible hard work, owing to their carrying such a press of sail in order to make as rapid passages as possible, and sustain the ship's reputation for speed." Unlike seamen on more leisurely vessels, who might reef the sails and then go below to ride out a storm, packet seamen had to stay on the job no matter what the weather might bring; in the winter months, the likely fare was banshee winds, blinding snow and mountainous seas that kept the decks awash for hours at a time. "Packet sailors," one captain wrote, "were the toughest class of men in all respects. They could stand the worst weather, food, and usage, and put up with less sleep, more rum and harder knocks than any other sailors."

Former packet crewman Melville had another observation. "There are classes of men in the world who bear the same relation to society at large that the wheels do to a coach: and are just as indispensable," he wrote. "Now, sailors form one of these wheels."

It took from two to three dozen such hardy men to sail a packet across the Atlantic. The crews were directed by three officers: the captain, and a first and second mate. The ship's company included a carpenter, a cook, a boatswain (who had charge of general maintenance), a few ship's boys in their teens (they did general errands for the first mate and learned the craft of sailing alongside the seamen), and a steward or two to attend to the needs of the passengers. But the major part of the ship's company consisted of seamen classified as able or ordinary, according to their experience.

An ordinary seaman did the tedious work of hauling ropes on deck, and running aloft to furl and reef the sails as ordered; he also took the wheel at times. An able seaman was the master of many arts. He not only had to know all about the intricate workings of sails, spars and ropes, he also had to be a bit of a blacksmith to make hooks and rings for the blocks, and more than a bit of a carpenter to make a jury mast out of a yard in an emergency. He had to be a weaver, able to work rope yarn into mats for securing and protecting jury spars, small boats and other shipboard paraphernalia. And for all his toughness, he had to have in his fingers the dexterity of an embroiderer, to work collars of hempen lace about the shrouds to secure them in place.

The crew was divided into two watches that served in alternation, each under the command of one of the mates, and each with a variety of duties to perform. Day and night, a seaman stood at the helm, keeping the ship on the course set by the captain. In stormy weather, when the vessel pitched and yawed, two men might be needed to hold the wheel, and both of them were often in danger of being swept overboard by the waves—sometimes 12 or 14 feet high—that washed over the stern. At least one crewman had to stand at the bow to keep a constant eye out for signs of changes in the weather, other ships, icebergs or land. Although the lookout's job was pleasant enough in fair weather, it had to be done in rain, snow and sleet and blistering sun alike.

For the rest, crewing a packet was largely a matter of endless maintenance chores. The tasks themselves were like those on any ship, but the demands of packet sailing gave maintenance special urgency. As Melville remembered his introduction to shipboard work, he was handed a bucket and ordered to slush the main topmast—rub it down with galley grease to prevent it from drying out. "It was a heavy bucket," he wrote, "with strong iron hoops, and might have held perhaps two gallons. But it was only half full now of a sort of thick lobbered gravy, which I afterward learned was boiled out of the salt beef used by the sailors. Upon getting into the rigging, I found it was no easy job to carry this heavy bucket up with me. The rope handle of it was so slippery with

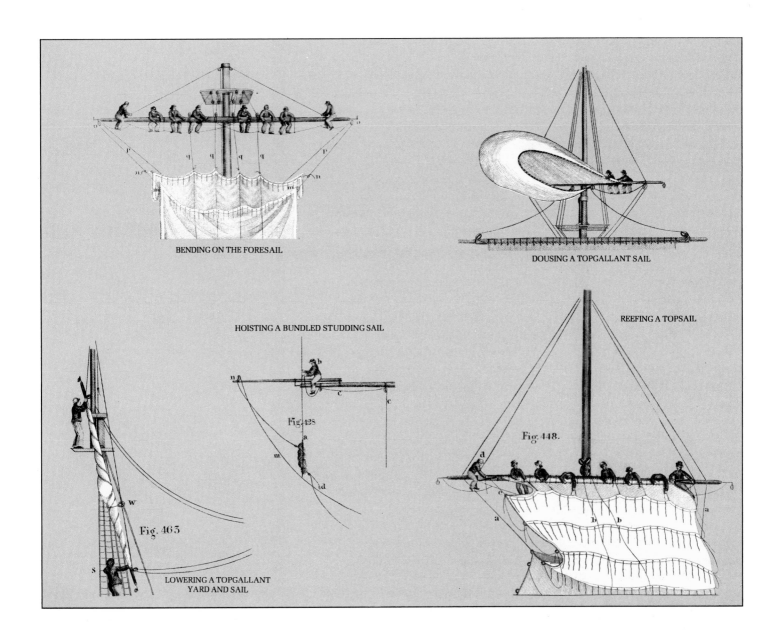

BENDING ON THE FORESAIL

DOUSING A TOPGALLANT SAIL

HOISTING A BUNDLED STUDDING SAIL

REEFING A TOPSAIL

Fig. 428

Fig. 465

Fig. 448.

LOWERING A TOPGALLANT
YARD AND SAIL

Five sketches from an 1819 manual on practical seamanship—intended by its author to "induce many to study the profession"—show some of the sail-handling tasks performed by packet seamen. The neat execution seen here was less than the whole story: In a winter gale on the Atlantic, work aloft became a life-and-death struggle to control flailing canvas while hanging on to ropes or spars that were sheathed with ice.

grease that, although I twisted it several times about my wrist, it would be still twirling round and round, and slipping off."

Alternatively, a seaman might be handed a hammer and swung out over the prow in a bowline to chip the rust off the anchor. Or he might be set to picking apart old ropes to collect oakum, the loose fiber that was used for calking. There were always new belaying pins to be whittled (the constant friction of the ropes wore the pins down), and sails to be mended.

And day after day, again and again, the deck had to be swabbed or scoured with a mop or a block of sandstone to keep it clean. This most monotonous of the seamen's rituals commenced at the start of the morning watch, at 4 o'clock, and although every inch of the deck was scoured, some captains—no doubt solely for the purpose of keeping their men occupied—ordered the job repeated during the afternoon watch. A great tub was dragged out and filled with buckets of salt water scooped up from the sea. Everybody grabbed a broom and scrubbed, as the mate splashed water from the tub onto the deck. "I scrubbed away fore and aft, till my back was almost broke," Melville recalled, "for the brooms had uncommon short handles."

Well-drilled crews carried out their tasks with smooth efficiency. "I observed much and often upon the quietness as well as the matchless activity of the crew," wrote Frances Wright, an Englishwoman who traveled from Liverpool to New York aboard the Black Ball Line's *Amity* in 1818. "No scolding on the part of the captain, nor sulky looks on the part of the men." Even making allowances for some romantic hyperbole on her part, the fact is that seamen more often than not took their demanding and endless work in stride. The occasional seaman who loafed through shipboard duties or performed them clumsily was known to his shipmates as a "sojer"—perhaps a throwback to the days when soldiers sailing to battle aboard warships were considered useless hands by veteran crewmen. The seaman who had mastered all aspects of his calling and practiced them skillfully was known to his colleagues simply as a "sailor man," and the language of the sea contained no higher compliment.

But for all the hard work a sailor did, he might well be a dandy. One seaman drew a vivid verbal picture of the type: "He was dressed very tastefully, too, as if he knew he was a good-looking fellow." He wore a "new silk handkerchief round his neck, passed through one of the vertebral bones of a shark, highly polished and carved. His trousers were of clear white duck, and he sported a handsome pair of pumps, and a tarpaulin hat bright as a looking-glass, with a long black ribbon streaming behind, and getting entangled every now and then in the rigging; and he had gold anchors in his ears, and a silver ring on one of his fingers, which was very much worn and bent from pulling ropes."

Both to help ease the ennui and to aid in coordination, seamen performed their routine chores to the rhythm of sea chanteys. There were songs for all jobs: "long drag" chanteys like "Blow the Man Down," sung as an accompaniment to such slow tasks as raising a topsail yard, and "short drag" chanteys like "Haul the Bowline," sung when a rope had to be tightened in short, quick motions. The singing had an eerie effect in the middle of the ocean in the dead of night. Remembering the sound, Melville wrote: "I almost looked around for goblins." Some of the songs were centuries old, and much of the phrasing—although it might sound like gibberish to the untutored ear of the passenger—was understood by seamen the world over. Frequently, a chantey would be led by a sailor who had a knack for incorporating the idiosyncrasies of various crew members into the lyrics. Because such a man made the work tolerable and even agreeable, he tended to be popular both with his fellow crewmen and with his superiors.

Watches generally shifted every four hours, and while not on duty a sailor had little in the way of pleasure. Certainly there was none in the meals; two monotonous staples were salt beef and biscuit, and another was burgoo, a porridge made of cornmeal mush and molasses. In search of relaxation the seaman had only the minimal amenities of the forecastle to repair to. There he could catch a few hours of sleep on his bunk or loaf on his sea chest—the only other piece of furniture available to him—breathing in the smoke from filthy clay pipes and the stench from rancid oilskins and unwashed bodies under the light produced by a single sooty lamp. An occasional packet forecastle might be equipped with a library; one passenger who sailed aboard the Black Ball liner *Nestor* in 1822 recalled that off-duty seamen spent their time in the forecastle reading.

When a gale struck, a cry of "All hands!" rudely interrupted work and relaxation alike, and the men of both watches scrambled to attention. A dozen or more of them had to climb aloft and crawl out on the swaying yards and slippery ropes. There, struggling to reef the sails, a seaman would hover "like a judgment angel between heaven and earth," Melville wrote; "both hands free, with one foot in the rigging and one somewhere behind you in the air. The sail would fill out like a balloon, with a report like a small cannon, and then collapse and sink away into a handful." In the meantime, the ship plunged and reared mercilessly. If the yard or the topmast snapped off in a strong wind, it frequently carried several seamen with it. Records are scanty, but in the year 1853, thirteen packet sailors were flung overboard on the New York-Liverpool run alone.

The pay that a packet sailor received was poor compensation for the dangers and hardships of his life. The wages averaged $15 a month —paltry even in the early 19th Century. And once paid, the sailors quickly frittered away their money on drink and women in the pleasure dens of the waterfront Sailortowns on either side of the Atlantic (*pages 94-95*). Few seamen provided for their own futures, and until the founding of the Sailors' Snug Harbor on Staten Island in 1833 (*page 97*) a sailor was likely to end his days as a waterfront bum. The only enduring reward the average packet crewman received for his labors was pride in his seamanship and in his own powers of endurance. Packet sailors, one captain asserted, "would not sail in any other trade."

There was always the possibility, of course, that a sailor might rise to become a mate—and indeed, most of the packet officers were sprung from seamen's ranks. The second mate was only a trifle better off than the seamen themselves. All the sails, masts and rigging were his responsibility, and he had to climb aloft to tend to them with the crewmen. He also had some perquisites not available to the rest of the crew, however; he was addressed respectfully as "mister," and he lived aft with the captain and the first mate—although the best he could do at mealtime was eat the leftovers from their table.

The first mate, generally a man in his late twenties or early thirties when appointed, was responsible for the cargo; he supervised its stowage aboard while in the port of embarkation, and retained custody of it throughout the voyage. He also had to know enough navigation to determine the ship's position with the aid of a sextant and a chronometer, and he had to know enough about seamanship to take over the ship if the captain became incapacitated. The job was the major route to command. One out of every three first mates in the 1830s could look forward to becoming a packet captain. The

On the loose in Sailortown

By the time a ship had made the run between New York and Liverpool, every sailor aboard had a month's wages to burn—and a month's tensions to work off. He did both with reckless abandon and stubborn indifference to consequences. "After a long, hard passage the pleasures of one night's spree became magnified out of all proportion," wrote a journalist in 1897.

The inhabitants of Sailortown—or Fiddler's Green, as waterfronts were sometimes known—were all too eager to oblige. Even before a packet was moored, crimps were swarming all over her, importuning the crewmen to desert that ship for easier berths in another—and promising them orgiastic delights ashore in the meantime. Unscrupulous shipmasters looked the other way when their sailors went over the side; fewer mouths to feed and wages to pay while the ship was detained in port meant higher profits.

To pent-up seamen, the waterfront was a maze of beckoning pleasures— "dance houses, doxies and tapsters," wrote novelist Herman Melville, using 19th Century euphemisms for broth-els, prostitutes and barkeeps. Within an easy walk of the dock stood scores of taverns whose signboards were emblazoned with crossed harpoons, capstans and anchors, indicating that sailors were welcome within. Theaters nearby offered crewmen a variety of dubious entertainments.

A music hall in Liverpool reportedly specialized in passing around containers of something called oxide gas—probably nitrous oxide, or laughing gas—for the audience to sniff. A few deep breaths of the stuff made the patrons so euphoric that they provided their own floor show.

Cannily placed amid the establishments for roistering were pawnshops, identified by three gilded spheres near the door. Here, when his money ran out, the seaman might offer his pantaloons for the price of a drink.

Should the pleasures of the taproom pall, tattoo parlors offered something more permanent; their artists did a brisk business decorating torsos and limbs with all manner of declarations. One popular design was a large crucifix, touted with the promise that it would assure the seaman a Christian burial should his body wash up on some pagan beach.

The people who embraced the seaman in their eagerness to take his money proved fickle friends. When he grew rambunctious, they were quick to summon the law. And when he had no more possessions to pawn for cash, barkeeps instantly grew grim and distant—and often turned the seaman over to a crimp. In no time at all, the hapless sailor found himself aboard an outgoing ship that was in need of a crew; in the meantime barkeep and crimp made off with a fee that was paid by the captain—and deducted from the seaman's prospective wages.

To landlubbers, the spectacle of sailors ashore eternally drunk, broke or jailed was a source of some amusement, as reflected in the lighthearted series of lithographs shown here (with their original titles in capitals). First published in London in 1825, they were copied by a Philadelphia lithographer 20 years later, so well did they fit the image of Jack Tar in Sailortown on either side of the Atlantic.

IN SIGHT OF PORT. A quartet of sailors in search of a caper raise hats and kerchiefs as they head for the road that leads to a hilltop tavern.

CASTING ANCHOR. The four tars find a tavern promisingly named "The Ship," where the proprietress greets them with a knowing smile.

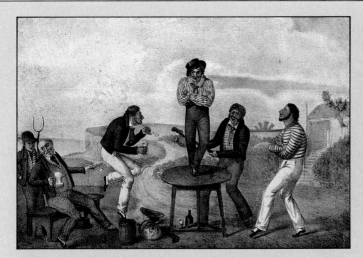

HALF SEAS OVER. *Loosened with grog, seamen dance a hornpipe while the tavern keeper, pleased with the fun, quiets a dour-looking bystander.*

RUN AGROUND WITH A STIFF BREEZE. *The tars show empty pockets to the proprietress—scowling now—as her husband peers from a window.*

AN ENGAGEMENT WITH A STORM. *As the tars become truculent, fists and furniture fly and a peg-legged customer hobbles out of the way.*

THE VICTORY. *Leaving "The Ship" a shambles, the jubilant seamen make off with the spoils of war: a couple of kegs of grog for the road.*

A DEAD CALM. *The tavern keeper—now bandaged—and the constable find the sailors sprawled in drunken oblivion beneath the tavern sign.*

PERFORMING QUARANTINE. *An officer of the law locks the rowdies in the brig as the crew of "The Ship" and the peg-legged veteran look on.*

remaining two thirds—if they had not made it by the age of 35—were apt to linger on in the job, becoming harsh disciplinarians of the sort known to crewmen as "bucko mates."

Few professions in the 19th Century world held more glamor—or promised more wealth—than that of packet captain. On both sides of the Atlantic, the captain enjoyed an elevated social status, mixing with wealthy businessmen, diplomats and other notables; William Brown, one of the most important bankers in Liverpool, made a regular habit of entertaining packet captains at dinner in one of the city's posh oyster-houses. The headlines of New York and Liverpool newspapers hailed the completion of a swift crossing, usually giving the captain equal billing with the ship. Bons vivants cultivated him, and small boys followed him on the street—keeping a respectful distance from the mighty man. Passengers frequently arranged their travel plans to coincide with the sailings of their favorite shipmasters.

Ashore in their own ports, the packet captains lived exceedingly well. Those who resided in New York owned opulent residences along the Battery and in Brooklyn Heights, on the opposite bank of the East River. Visiting captains stayed at such establishments as the elegant City Hotel.

And the shipmasters dressed as well as they lived. According to the boyhood memories of Julian Hawthorne—son of the novelist Nathaniel Hawthorne, who served as American consul in Liverpool from 1853 to 1857—the captains shared "a disposition to wear a high-colored necktie and a broad, gold watch-chain, and to observe a certain smartness in their boots and their general shore rigging."

A packet captain could afford to live and dress in style—not because of his salary (a mere $40 a month), but because he commanded a hefty share of the packet's profits. He took primage, or about 5 per cent of the income from the cargo; he also received 25 per cent of the passengers' fares; and he frequently got the whole fee for carrying mail. Altogether such proceeds could fetch him an enviable $5,000 a year—almost 30 times the earnings of a seaman.

Still, the captain earned every penny. No matter how much authority he might delegate to his mates, in the last analysis it was he who was responsible for judging how much punishment his ship could take and still sail safely at top speed. In racing other captains and his own record, he had to dare to leave every possible inch of canvas flying—and sometimes a sail might rip in two, or blow away altogether. A captain could not, however, risk serious damage to the ship, so he had to make hair-breadth decisions with a daring that would have amounted to recklessness had he not made them on the basis of unrelenting vigilance and profound knowledge.

No captain displayed greater skill or diligence than Nathaniel Brown Palmer, a product of the port town of Stonington, Connecticut, on Long Island Sound. Young Nat first shipped out to sea when he was 14 years old. The War of 1812 was then raging, and lively young New Englanders like Palmer found adventure in running a British blockade that extended from the east end of Long Island to within sight of Stonington.

After this rousing introduction to the sea, Palmer went on to sail

An anchorage for weary sea dogs

Snug Harbor's original buildings, sited to overlook New York's busy shipping channels, accommodated 200 sailors.

"They took me in because I was crippled, and washed and shaved me, and gave me a room as clean as the captain's cabin of a man-o-war, and said, 'There, you're safe an' sound forever!' " So say the memoirs of a retired sailor who might have died penniless on the streets—like thousands before him—had it not been for an institution called Sailors' Snug Harbor. Dedicated to the care of "aged, decrepit and worn-out sailors," it was founded on Staten Island in 1833 with funds bequeathed by shipowner John Randall.

Inside Snug Harbor, the destitute sailor—usually a veteran of Atlantic service—traded his life of hardships for one of unaccustomed leisure. The "Snugs," as the men were called, enjoyed hefty meals and slept on soft beds in cozy rooms. The retirement home had a full-time doctor, nurses, game rooms, and a library with all the latest newspapers. Its residents could earn spending money—sometimes as much as $75 per year—by weaving hammocks or carving ship models. The Snugs were even allowed to ferry into Manhattan, despite the likelihood that they would go on forbidden drinking sprees there.

For drinking on or off the premises, sailors were "tabooed"—denied such privileges as their tobacco ration, the use of the library or the chance to earn money—and not permitted to leave the grounds for days. Similar penalties were meted out to those who failed to attend church. But most seamen were only too happy to accept such mild discipline as the price of shelter and support in their declining years. When novelist Theodore Dreiser visited an 83-year-old resident of Snug Harbor and asked him to tell of his adventures at sea, the former sailor replied, "I could, but I would rather tell you of 13 peaceful years here."

aboard sealers that voyaged to Arctic waters and on cotton packets that sped between New York and New Orleans. By the age of 38, he was commander of the transatlantic packet *Garrick*—and part owner of the Dramatic Line to which she belonged.

In this role, he regularly exploited his seamanly talents with a bit of showmanship in New York harbor. By that time, the steam tugboat had already been invented, making the job of entering and exiting from a crowded harbor easier. But Palmer insisted on retaining the old ways and refused to make use of a tug to help him to and from a berth. While the ship was still tied up, he would come to the starboard side of the quarter-deck and bellow into a trumpet, ordering the topsails and jibs hoisted and the spanker loosened. The sails would catch the wind and then, just as the lines began to strain, he would order them cast off. The packet would back into the river, where her stern was turned upstream by nimble shifting of the jibs and the topsails. When the vessel was clear of the pier, she was headed toward the sea. All the lighter sails spread quickly, and as the crowds on the waterfront shouted hoarse farewells, Captain Nat—as he was known—took his ship down the bay. On his return to port he repeated the process in reverse.

Palmer's stamina matched his seamanship. One admirer, describing him on a typical passage from New York to Liverpool, wrote that Palmer paced the quarter-deck day and night, giving commands, support and encouragement to the helmsman and to the crewmen in the rigging. Only occasionally did he sit down—and then in an armchair secured under the weather rail—to take coffee and food when the steward pressed them on him, or to catch a few moments of rest now and then. Hardly ever going below, he kept in physical contact with his ship and the sea throughout the voyage.

Prior to the advent of the packet ship and the compulsion for speed, sailing ships had tended to idle at night, shortening sail and keeping the number of crewmen on watch to a minimum. Not so the packets. "Night is the time to try the nerve and make quick passages," one captain remembered. "The best ship-masters that I had sailed with were those who were most on deck after dark, and relied upon nobody but themselves to carry canvas." In speed as in so much else, Palmer was the paragon; sailing from Liverpool to New York in 1840, he brought the *Siddons* into port in 15 days, a record for the westward crossing that was never broken by another packet.

Pushing a ship hard—even if not so relentlessly as Nat Palmer did—was such a strain that the average packet captain lasted only five years on the transatlantic run. If a captain showed signs of slowing down—missing schedules or even failing to match records—the shipowners fired him. But many captains came ashore voluntarily and either retired on their savings or took up such occupations as inspecting ships for marine insurance companies or serving as consultants to shipbuilders.

One long-lived exception to the general rule was Captain Charles H. Marshall, a gruff, square-jawed, aggressive master who put in a total of 27 years at sea, 12 of them as a packet captain. Marshall came from a line of Nantucket whaling men. But the Revolutionary War had interrupted the whaling industry, and when Marshall was born in a 15-by-18-foot log cabin in 1792, his father was farming 100 acres in the village of Easton in upstate New York. At the age of 15, with a borrowed $13, a sea chest, a ham, a loaf of bread, a pie and some crackers, young Marshall reasserted the family tradition by shipping out on a Nantucket whaler.

Nine years later, at the age of 24, he became captain of the *Julius Caesar*, a 350-ton merchantman with a crew of 12. Carrying a cargo of cotton from Charleston to Liverpool, he challenged himself to race the merchantman *Martha*, which had left port a full day ahead of him under the command of Captain Beau Glover, a social lion ashore and a hard driver at sea. This was prior to the advent of the scheduled packet with her need for speed, but even then Marshall could not resist an opportunity to demonstrate how fast he could make a ship go.

It was March, and the Atlantic was surly. Captain Marshall nevertheless commanded his 12 crewmen to hoist every sail in the ship's locker, and he managed to reach the head of St. George's Channel between Ireland and England in just 18 days. The channel was closed in with fog, but still Marshall left on as much sail as he dared, and made the mouth of the Mersey River on the 22nd day—18 hours ahead of the *Martha*. The owners of the *Julius Caesar*—who were bound to benefit from their ship's reputation for speed—rewarded their captain with a new suit tailored in London.

Six years later, in 1822, Marshall joined the Black Ball Line as a packet captain, and he sailed the Atlantic in that capacity until 1834, when he bought control of the line and took up residence in New York to run it. Marshall had four seafaring brothers, and they were just as durable; when all five met for a reunion in Easton, in 1851, they calculated that among them they had spent 97 years at sea and had made more than 300 Atlantic crossings. Charles alone earned a fortune of $150,000, demonstrating the heights to which a packet captain could rise.

Once in a while a captain might find himself battling not the elements, but his own crewmen. Not even a popular captain was immune; tough crews sometimes liked to see just how far they could press a resolute commander. When faced with mutiny, the captain had to use every resource at his command—humor, persuasion, insistence, threats—and, as a last resort, force. The odds were that he would win, but a mutinous crew, or even a crew soured by a single troublesome member, could make the struggle close.

The year 1832 saw a mutiny that, in the manner of its resolution, surely stands alone in the annals of seafaring. It occurred aboard the

The 895-ton Dramatic liner Garrick reduces sail at the entrance to Liverpool harbor. Nicknamed Speedy Garrick, she once completed the westbound passage in an astonishing 18 days. During a fierce storm in 1841, she ran aground off Deal, New Jersey, and was almost totally wrecked, but she was restored in a few months and sailed the Atlantic for another 12 years.

packet *Sheffield* when she was anchored in the Mersey River, just about ready to sail. As a result of some brouhaha whose details are tantalizingly obscure, the crew grew rough and terrorized the passengers, who fled to their cabins and locked themselves inside. As it happened, the captain was ashore on last-minute business. But luckily for him and the ship, he got aid from the least likely person aboard: his 20-year-old bride. The only person to keep a cool head, she helped herself to a pair of pistols from his quarters and, with one in each hand, strode on deck, threatening to shoot the first crewman who made another move. Doubtless stunned by the sight of this floating Annie Oakley, they stood as they were—and the captain conveniently arrived moments later to take charge. He sent the mutineers ashore and rounded up another crew.

A much more prolonged ordeal took place in 1859 aboard the packet *Dreadnought*, a palatial 1,400-tonner that was the cynosure of her day. She was captained by Samuel Samuels, a man so engaging that cabin passengers had to make their reservations an entire season in advance to be assured a place on board his ship. Sailors liked him too, but they quickly dubbed the *Dreadnought* the "Wild Ship of the Atlantic" for the headlong passages she made under his command. Samuels

The Yankee who wrote the mariners' bible

Bowditch reposes in his study beneath a bust of Pierre Laplace.

In all the history of sea travel, no man did more to tame the empty expanses of the oceans than Nathaniel Bowditch, a Yankee genius who simplified the procedure for determining longitude and who compiled the first reliable manual on celestial navigation. Before Bowditch's day, navigating by the sun, stars and moon had been an abstruse and uncertain art; after he published his great work, it could be mastered by any mariner.

Bowditch was born in 1773 in the seafaring town of Salem, Massachusetts, the son of an impoverished cooper. After sporadic schooling, he was apprenticed to a ship chandler when he was 12 years old, but he found time to teach himself mathematics, astronomy and—the better to read scientific books—Latin, the first of more than 24 languages he learned in his lifetime.

At 22, spindly in appearance and prematurely gray, Bowditch went to sea as a ship's clerk on a merchantman. He would make five far-ranging commercial voyages in all, the last one—when he was 29—as a commander. The practical challenge of ocean travel bore instant fruit. At the time, the usual method for finding longitude was by a laborious series of computations based on sightings of the moon. Bowditch tried his hand at the system, pondered its flaws, and developed tables that eliminated several steps in the calculations, greatly speeding the task.

was so confident he could keep his schedules that he made shippers a unique offer: He would forfeit the freight charges if he did not deliver on time. As far as is known, this bold promise never cost him a penny; he made such rapid crossings that sailors were heard to remark that Captain Samuels had a "secret ocean path between New York and Liverpool."

As he recounted in colorful memoirs entitled *From the Forecastle to the Cabin*, Samuels had worked his way up to captain through the ranks. "My stepmother and I had such differences that a house the size of the capitol at Washington would not have been large enough to hold us both," he wrote, and so he "took French leave of home" at the age of 11 and shipped out as a cabin boy and cook on a schooner. That was in the year 1833. The sea suited him well, and in 10 years—at the age of 21— he was captain and nominal owner of a full-rigged ship that carried refined sugar from Amsterdam to Genoa.

By the 1840s, when the Liverpool packets were in their glory years, Samuels had become a veteran with firsthand experience in every phase of sailing a ship. He knew well the rigors and dangers encountered by seamen, for he had done every job required of them. In the course of so doing, he had withstood many a mishap: He had fallen

While at sea, Bowditch methodically checked his own figures for longitude against the charts and tables of the day, most notably *The Practical Navigator*, a widely used manual by an English mathematician named John Moore. He found more than 8,000 errors in Moore's work—some of them evidently responsible for shipwrecks.

At the urging of a Massachusetts publisher, he produced a revised version that, in addition to corrected tables, included maps of the night sky, information on winds and currents, and even a seamen's glossary. In 1802, the book was published under his own name as *The New American Practical Navigator*. Soon known simply as "Bowditch," it was a phenomenal success. Mariners the world over clamored for a copy, and ultimately the publishing rights were purchased by the U.S. government. Much revised (Bowditch himself oversaw nine editions during his lifetime), it is still in use today.

Bowditch did not limit the application of his talents to celestial navigation. He went on to run insurance companies in Salem and Boston, and to write on subjects ranging from the orbit of comets to the harbors of Massachusetts. He spent his last years translating the works of the era's greatest astronomer, Pierre Laplace of France. But he would always be most revered at sea. After his death in 1838, flags were lowered to half-mast in harbors around the globe.

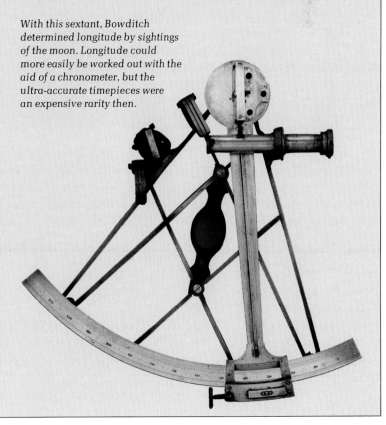

With this sextant, Bowditch determined longitude by sightings of the moon. Longitude could more easily be worked out with the aid of a chronometer, but the ultra-accurate timepieces were an expensive rarity then.

overboard on the Bahama Bank while reefing a sail, weathered a typhoon in the China Sea, endured a grounding in the Dardanelles and fought pirates in the Mediterranean. He had also earned a reputation for being a dead shot with either hand.

Assuming command of the *Dreadnought* was Samuels' crowning achievement; indeed, the Red Cross Line, founded in 1843, had the packet built for him. When sailing the *Dreadnought*, he took along his wife—a privilege that was granted to all packet captains, but one that few of them exercised. Partly as a courtesy to her and her sensibilities, he banned swearing on board the ship (an order that was hardly likely to be obeyed), instituted compulsory evening prayers, and flew the flags of the United States and the Red Cross Line during the Sunday services. Generally a ship's flags remained in the locker except when another vessel hove into view. When a passenger asked one Sunday, "Why are the flags hoisted, when there are no ships in sight to see them?" Mrs. Samuels sweetly rejoined: "God sees them."

Such piety was not likely to influence tough seamen, but Samuels liked his crews tough, and he took great pride in his ability to handle them. "I never rejected a crew or a part of one on account of their bad character," he claimed. "I generally found among these men the toughest and best sailors. I frequently had a number of the 'Bloody Forties,' as they styled themselves, among the crew." The Bloody Forties was a gang of about 40 Liverpool men who had been sailing together for years, and long comradeship in the demanding conditions of packet sailing had filled them with braggadocio. Their ringleader was an especially hardened fellow known as Finnigan, and they claimed to have killed a captain at his prompting during one of their voyages. Now they were to give Samuels his sternest trial as a commander.

On July 11, 1859, the *Dreadnought* weighed anchor in Liverpool with a cargo of iron bars and a number of German emigrants aboard. Finnigan and the Bloody Forties were among the crew, and Captain Samuels had been warned that they intended to mutiny; in a certain Mrs. Riley's tavern on the Liverpool waterfront, Finnigan had been heard inciting the men "to clip the wings of the bloody old *Dreadnought* and give the skipper a swim."

Before the day was out, Samuels knew that trouble was brewing. At noon, off Queenstown, the helmsman failed to acknowledge a "Steer steady" order to Samuels' satisfaction. "The impertinent tone of his voice caused me to jump towards him," Samuels wrote. "He attempted to draw his sheath-knife. Seeing my danger, I struck the man, knocking him senseless leeward of the wheel. Wallace, my dog, then took charge of him, and kept his fore paws on his chest. I took the knife from him, and called the officers to handcuff him. He was then put in the afterhouse, and locked up."

Samuels entrusted the helm to the third mate, a Mr. Whitehorn, who had been sailing with him for years. The captain then issued a command to the crew at large. "Turn to, and haul taut the weather mainbrace," he ordered. Not one man moved.

By now, word of trouble aboard had spread to the passengers. For safety's sake Samuels ordered them below. He went to his cabin to get his

Captain Charles H. Marshall, who commanded three vessels for the Black Ball Line, crossed the Atlantic an astonishing 94 times. Retiring ashore at the age of 42, he bought into the firm and managed it for the next 30 years.

pistols and cutlass, which he concealed beneath a raglan cloak and then carried back on deck, with his dog Wallace trotting alongside him.

He was walking past the water cask by the galley door when the crewmen rushed at him with their knives. "The time had come," Samuels decided, "for me to prove to these men that moral courage was superior to brute force. With a pistol in each hand, pointed at the heads of those nearest to me, and a cutlass at my side, I stood immovable. The screaming of the women and children below, blended with the noise on deck, beggars all description. Not a man dared to come nearer than about 12 feet from me, knowing that another step forward would seal his doom." But Finnigan bared his breast and dared Samuels to shoot him, calling the captain "an outrageous name."

Samuels stood fast, and both sides settled down to a siege. Samuels ordered the food cut off from the mutineers. As for himself, he paced the deck throughout the night, together with Wallace and the three mates.

At seven bells (3:30 a.m.), the captain made another appeal to reason, with no better results. At noon the breeze freshened and he commanded in a voice that could be heard fore and aft: "Take in the royals," the sails that were used when the winds were steady and favorable. The command was acknowledged with an equally firm "Go to hell!"

With too much canvas set, the ship was soon tearing through the water at a speed of 12 knots, pitching and burying her forecastle and sending spray from the weather bow up over the captain's head. With the assistance of his mates, he might have lowered the sails, but he dared not, for four men alone could never have hoisted them again; on a 1,400-ton ship, that was a job requiring close to a dozen men.

On the second morning without breakfast the men began to show signs of yielding; they offered to turn to if they were fed first. "You shall work before you eat," the captain responded. They declined, and the siege continued.

The German passengers, confined below, had only the faintest idea of what was at stake, and thought the captain was being too hard on the men. During the second day a delegation of passengers approached him, asking him to let the mutineers have some food. He refused, warning: "If they conquer me they will scuttle the ship, after having committed the greatest outrages on those whom you hold most dear; and at night, while you are asleep, the hatches will be battened down and the ship sunk, while they will take to the boats." That quieted the passengers.

By sunset at the end of the second day, 56 hours had passed without sleep for the captain and his officers, or food for the mutineers. Samuels decided to enlist the passengers in his service. He went into the after steerage and asked them to join him in quelling the mutiny.

According to his account, they responded as one man: "Order us, Captain, and we will obey." Samuels promptly armed 17 of them with iron bars taken from the cargo, placed four men in ambush behind the pigpen, and strategically scattered the rest about the deck.

The night passed in silent tension, while Samuels waited for the mutineers to make their move. Around midnight, as he stood watch on the quarter-deck, his faithful dog Wallace suddenly gave a growl. Two men had crawled as far as the capstan, 20 feet or so away. It turned out they

A man-made artery into the continent

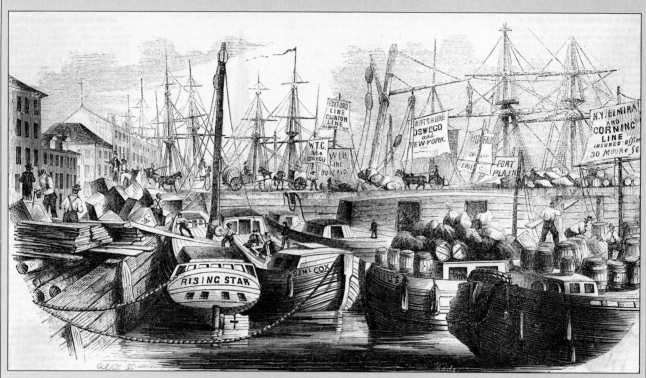

At a Manhattan dock, canal barges are loaded with westbound cargoes. Steamers towed the barges up the Hudson to Albany.

One year before packet service across the Atlantic came into being, work began on the Erie Canal, a threadlike inland waterway that would give a disproportionate boost to the transocean trade. The canal aimed at nothing less than opening the West: It would link Buffalo on the Great Lakes with Albany on the Hudson River, thus allowing the port of New York to exchange goods with an enormous sweep of territory extending almost halfway across the continent.

Proposals for a waterway through upstate New York had surfaced as early as 1800. But the difficulties were immense. Some 360 miles separated Buffalo and Albany, including sizable tracts of swamp and forest. Any canal between the two points would have to contain locks to overcome the 565-foot elevation difference, as well as aqueducts to carry the canal over rivers.

The project began to receive serious attention when New York City's Mayor DeWitt Clinton pressed its commercial advantages in letters to newspapers and in a petition to the legislature. In 1817, the state legislature agreed to provide financial backing, and for the next eight years an army of several thousand men labored steadily at the great enterprise. When the canal was finally finished in October 1825, Clinton made the inaugural voyage from Buffalo to New York, where he poured a cask of Lake Erie water into the Atlantic to symbolize the "wedding of the waters."

The marriage proved singularly felicitous. During the first year, 218,000 tons of cargo moved along the canal; 25 years later, the figure was 3,076,617 tons. Settlers from as far away as Lake Superior sent flour, timber, whiskey and livestock down the waterway and on to New York for shipment to coastal markets or across the ocean. And with the sale of their produce, Western farmers could now afford to import manufactured goods from Europe.

Accompanying this freight were tens of thousands of emigrants, who had heard about the easy access to America's interior. Every day hundreds of emigrants reached New York, and many of them continued up the Hudson to the canal, crammed together into squat barges. So heavy was the passenger traffic that residents along the route "must have frequently thought that Europe was moving to this country," observed an upstate editor in 1847.

After 1850, the canal began to lose traffic to the railroads, which offered faster service to the West. But by then, it had surpassed its promoters' wildest dreams. Tolls had paid off the state's original seven-million-dollar investment within a decade, and the canal deserved much of the credit for the prosperity of the packet lines and for giving the port of New York a commanding lead over its East Coast rivals.

were not there to fight, however, but to surrender. They informed the captain that some of the others had planned to launch an attack on the galley in the morning.

At daybreak, as Samuels was taking a reconnoitering stroll along the starboard side of the galley, accompanied by Whitehorn and Wallace, Wallace suddenly growled again. Instantly two of the mutineers leaped at Samuels, their knives drawn. The captain leveled his pistol at one of them, and Wallace made for the other's throat.

The other mutineers rushed in next, only to be met by the Germans, swinging their iron bars. The ruffians retreated to the starboard side forward, where Samuels again leveled his pistol and thundered: "Death to the first man who dares advance! I will give you one moment to throw your knives overboard!"

"You shall be the first to go, you damned psalm-singing ----" Finnigan began. But he had lost his support. One by one the mutineers threw down their knives. Samuels demanded an apology from Finnigan, but did not get one, so he dealt the mutineer a blow that sent him headlong down the forecastle.

When Finnigan regained consciousness, Samuels had him shackled and thrown into the sweatbox—a narrow box kept aboard practically all ships for punishment of insubordinate seamen. "In less than half an hour," Samuels recalled, Finnigan "cried out for mercy, and was ready to say or do anything to be let out of irons." By this time Samuels had ordered the cook to dispense coffee to the crew, and had put them to work scouring the quarter-deck. Before them all, reported Samuels, the repentant Finnigan declared: "Captain, I have had enough. To say this does not make a coward of a man when he has found his master."

Indeed, there was nothing that a seaman admired more than a resolute captain. After the ship had docked, the ex-mutineers gathered on deck, hats in hand, and crowded around Samuels to pay him homage. Clearly the occasion called for a speech, and Samuels was not the man to avoid the challenge. "Let me say that I would trust any of you hereafter with my life," he told them. "I never had or expect to have a better set of sailors with me." The crew, if Samuels' account is to be believed, responded with "God bless you, Captain," as they left the *Dreadnought*.

So ends a tale that—for all its shameless hyperbole—reflects the strength of will and mastery of men that packet sailing demanded of every captain.

By the time of Captain Samuels' career, packet ships and their reliable schedules had long since become an established fact of transatlantic commerce. Indeed, it had taken scarcely a decade to happen. Merchants and passengers had come to rely on them. So had the nation's officials; in 1828 the duties that were collected on cargoes arriving in New York were estimated to be enough to pay the entire cost of running the United States government. But the packets were more important than the profits the owners made on them or the revenues the government collected from them. By keeping to their schedules year in and year out, in spite of all the perils the Atlantic had to offer, they had changed forever the habits of the commercial shipping industry.

Liverpool—the pacesetter among ports

A row of flagstaffs winds past the Bidstone Hill Observatory outside Liverpool; when inbound vessels were spotted at the entrance to the Mersey, flags were raised to alert the owners.

"Sailors love this Liverpool," wrote American novelist Herman Melville after visiting the port as a packet crewman in 1839; "here they find their Paradise." Brothels and dance halls beckoned on all sides, and gin palaces specialized in putting on lewd shows known as "free and easies." Melville himself was more inclined to view the city as hell. It was, he said, infested with "land-sharks, land-rats, and other vermin, which make the hapless mariner their prey."

Like it or not, the seaman who crossed the Atlantic in midcentury had a better-than-even chance of landing in Liverpool—for the very good reason that its 200-acre dock system on the Mersey River was unrivaled anywhere in the world. Liverpool's maritime facilities were essentially the creation of one man, Jesse Hartley, an engineer who devoted 36 years to the service of the city. Between 1824 and 1860 he designed 28 new docks. He equipped them with swing bridges that opened to admit ships and closed to allow pedestrian and horse-drawn traffic to move freely along the waterfront (pages 108-109). He lined the docks with fireproof warehouses where goods could be stored and protected from pilferage or spoilage while awaiting transshipment. Hartley also installed a telegraph system for the convenience of Liverpool merchants.

Though most of Liverpool's civic improvements were aimed at fostering trade, the welfare of the seamen themselves was given some thought: By the middle of the 19th Century, social reformers had begun to build hostels, almshouses and churches for sailors. But for every such effort to help or uplift Jack Tar, a welter of temptations pulled in the opposite direction. Of drinking dens alone, Liverpool had more than 2,000 in 1840—perhaps the highest concentration in the world.

Hundreds of sailing vessels occupy the spacious docks along the Mersey in a panoramic view of Liverpool drawn in 1847. One Liverpool shipowner counted 300 ships arriving on a single tide.

Off-duty seamen lounge on a swing bridge by one of the fortress-like gates that Jesse Hartley designed for the Liverpool waterfront. Gatekeepers worked inside the towers in shifts, recording the ships that entered and left the docks, and cranking winches that swung the bridges aside to allow vessels to pass.

Liverpool's Customs House overlooks a quay where stevedores have gathered to moor an incoming packet. By the second quarter of the 19th Century, customs revenues approached two million pounds per year—much of it slated to finance the constant expansion of the waterfront.

Packet ships arrive in a Liverpool dock basin to unload their cargo at warehouses. Such buildings—fireproof because they were made of brick and cast iron and contained no lumber—were favored with reduced rates by insurance companies.

Built in 1846, the Sailor's Home was one of several Liverpool hostels intended, said a group of merchants and clergymen, to "improve the conditions of life of British Seamen, and to arrest them from corrupting influences." Unfortunately, few of the managers shared the idealism of the home's founders, and the lodgings quickly became filthy and crowded.

Three buildings belonging to the Seamen's Hospital overlook a Liverpool fairground. The facility—actually an almshouse for destitute sailors and their families—was also known as the "sixpenny hospital" because all sailors coming into port were required to give sixpence of their wages for its upkeep.

In front of the Mariner's Church, a ship that was converted into a chapel for seamen in 1826, a city vendor hawks her wares while fashionable Liverpudlians stroll along the dock. The floating church could hold hundreds of worshippers —but few sailors came aboard to worship.

Chapter 4

Running a gantlet of nautical perils

y the very nature of their trade, packet captains had to take risks that other seamen shunned. A fixed schedule and speed of transit were the hallmarks of these vessels, and packet owners would not long tolerate a skipper who let weather delay his departure or who failed to drive his ship to the utmost. These stern rules of regularity and speed, imposed on the stormiest ocean in the world, frequently resulted in tragedy. It was perhaps an augury of sorts that the first time the sea claimed a packet, it did so with apocalyptic violence. What happened to the Black Ball Line's *Albion* in 1822 was the dark side of the Atlantic shuttle, the grim obverse of its princely profits and seafaring panache.

When the *Albion* sailed out of New York harbor on the afternoon of April 1, there was every reason to expect a safe passage. The 434-ton packet was designed for rugged conditions; among other fortifying features, she had iron knees tying her ribs to the deck beams. The *Albion* had also compiled an enviable record for speed during her three years of service. Only once had she encountered trouble. The year before, she had run aground near Liverpool, but after unloading some cargo and waiting through a few changes of tide, she had floated free, none the worse for the incident.

If the *Albion* had much to be said for her, so did her captain. John Williams was 37 years old and already at the top of his profession. Although he stood only five feet five and a half inches tall, he possessed vigor and confidence that more than made up for whatever he lacked in size. Williams had been one of the Black Ball Line's four original captains, and now he was the fleet's unofficial commodore. He was also worth $16,000—a small fortune at the time—and was about to add handsomely to that sum. In addition to her officers and her 22 crewmen, the *Albion* was carrying 23 cabin passengers and six more passengers in steerage. The cabin fares alone totaled $3,079.97, of which the captain's share came to $1,646.64. Part of the money had already been spent on food and wine for the passengers to consume en route, but Captain Williams expected to clear some $1,300 for about three weeks' work.

Little is known about the passengers. Those in steerage included a Stephen Chase of Canada; Dr. Carver, a veterinarian; Mr. Harrison, a carpenter; and Mr. Baldwin, a cotton spinner from Yorkshire. Of the cabin passengers, a certain Miss Powell—the daughter of the Honorable W. D. Powell, Chief Justice of Upper Canada—was described by a shipmate as having "unusual charm." Another cabin passenger, Charles Lefevbre-Desnouettes, was a quiet Frenchman who had an air of mystery about him. In fact, he possessed a fascinating past. A former general under Napoleon and a count of the Empire, he had lost his title and had

Small craft from a nearby settlement rush to the aid of a passenger ship hard aground off the New England coast. These waters, menacing mariners with shifting shoals, dense fogs and sudden storms, claimed more ships and lives than any other portion of the packets' routes.

been condemned to death after the Emperor's overthrow in 1815. Leaving his wife in France, he had fled to the United States. Now, responding to his wife's pleas and encouraged by the intercession of the French Minister in Washington, he was returning home to explore the possibility of repatriation. Strangely enough, one of Lefevbre-Desnouettes's fellow cabin passengers was a British officer who had fought against the Frenchman in Spain; Major William Gough, of the 68th Regiment of the Line, had been wounded in that campaign.

The crossing was agreeably uneventful, marked by "moderate and favorable" weather, as First Mate Henry Cammyer later recalled. Landfall was made shortly after noon on April 21, near Fastnet Rock at the southwestern tip of Ireland. The 21 days it had taken the *Albion* to sail from New York to Ireland was excellent time and, as a passenger named William Everhart would remember, "all hands flattered themselves that in a short time they should reach their destined harbor." Fastnet Rock came into view at 1:30 p.m., bearing east-northeast and roughly nine miles away. Half an hour later, the lookout sighted Cape Clear, the next important landmark. But visibility was fast diminishing now. Conditions were "thick and foggy," recalled First Mate Cammyer. Suddenly heavy squalls hit, driving the ship directly toward the rocky coast.

Captain Williams swung the vessel to a new course, east-southeast—"carrying all prudent sail to crowd the ship off the land," Cammyer reported, but keeping the topsails double-reefed. It was little use; this was no ordinary storm. About 4 o'clock, gusts carried away the foreyard and split the fore-topsail. As night approached, the winds reached hurricane force. At 8:30 the *Albion* was struck by a monstrous wave that threw the vessel on her beam-ends, injuring many passengers and carrying away the mainmast, the head of the mizzenmast and the fore-topmast. The deck was swept clear of boats, deckhouse, bulwarks, compasses and wheel. The sea stove in all the hatches, William Everhart later said, "so that every wave which passed over her ran into the hold without anything to stop it." Finishing its work, this enormous, deadly wave casually swept overboard six members of the crew and one of the cabin passengers, a Mr. Converse from Troy, New York.

Along with everything else on deck, all of the ship's axes had been lost to the sea, so that the tangled wreckage of the masts could not be chopped away. Not that it made much difference. Without a wheel, the ship was uncontrollable, a bit of flotsam being swept toward the shore by the howling winds.

Captain Williams was magnificent. He gave his orders "steadily and coolly," Everhart remembered, and enlisted the able-bodied men among the passengers in the job of manning the pumps. The men responded eagerly to the suggestion—and Miss Powell begged to join them. The assignment was exhausting. The *Albion* bucked so violently in the fury of the storm that the workers had to be lashed to the pumps in order to keep from being washed away as they struggled to keep up with the seas flooding the ship. "All who could do no good on deck retired below," Everhart wrote, "but the water was knee-deep in the cabin, and the furniture floating about rendered the situation dangerous and dreadful." The captain must have known the terrible odds against them, but he did

As a few lucky passengers and crewmen wait to be rescued from ledges they managed to reach, the packet ship Albion splits asunder on the rocks of the Irish coast in 1822. Some 45 lives were lost.

his best to cheer everyone with the hope that the wind might shift before daybreak. In the meantime, the high Irish cliffs waited.

Around 1 o'clock in the morning, the light on the Old Head of Kinsale became visible. An hour later the crashing of waves on the rocks signaled the approaching end. Captain Williams called all the passengers up on deck. Many had broken bones and other injuries; Lefevbre-Desnouettes had suffered a broken arm and extensive bruises. Williams told them briefly that the ship was doomed. Some of the women shrieked in terror. "Our situation at that moment was indescribable," the first mate said afterward. "I can scarcely dwell upon, much less attempt to detail, its horrors." In the best Army tradition, Major Gough reminded the men that "death, come as he would, was an unwelcome messenger, but they must meet him like men."

At 3 a.m. the *Albion* struck a rock at the foot of the Kinsale cliffs. "The next wave threw her further on the rock," Everhart reported, "the third further still, until, nearly balanced, she swung around, and her stern was

At the entrance to Liverpool harbor, packets struggle to survive in a hurricane that struck on January 7, 1839. More than 60 vessels—most of them tied up at piers—were damaged or sunk during the epic storm, which raged for two days.

driven against another, near the shore. In this situation, every wave was making a complete break over her, many were drowned on deck." Williams labored valiantly to save his passengers, but soon after the ship struck, he was swept away by a wave, never to reappear. An Irishman looking down from the cliffs at this time saw five bodies lying on deck and "four other fellow creatures, calling out for assistance, without our being able to render them any." Then a final wave crashed, and the ship broke apart. Everhart and a few others near the stern were not immediately washed away, but those near the bow were lost.

Just before the ship split asunder, the first mate and six of the crew had scrambled onto some rocks at the base of the cliffs. Everhart and the others with him now managed to do the same. In the surging breakers Everhart clung steadfastly to his perch; some of those around him, however, were too weak or too injured to struggle for long against the power of the sea. Several hours passed before the storm abated enough to enable rescuers to lower a rope and haul the survivors to safety. Later, people who lived nearby went down to see what was left of the ship's cargo. A box containing £5,000 in cash remained intact, but little else. Bales of cotton and the contents of ruptured mailbags were strewn far and wide, mingling with the corpses that washed ashore. Of the 23 cabin passengers, William Everhart was the only one to survive. The steerage passenger Stephen Chase was also saved, as were the first mate and six members of the crew. But 45 souls, from Captain Williams to the exiled Lefevbre-Desnouettes and the ship's boys, all perished—a loss of life that would not be exceeded in the packet trade for another 25 years.

The wreck of the *Albion* savagely undercut some of the romance that had been gathering around packets: Swift and tough as they were, they enjoyed no special immunity from the Atlantic's wrath. That lesson would be driven home by many another tragedy during the five decades that these sailing ships shuttled between the Old World and the New: One packet in six came to a disastrous end.

At times, as if to prove there was no limit to its ruthlessness, the sea claimed multiple victims with a single blow. Such was the case in January 1839, when England's western coast was pounded by a hurricane so violent that trees several miles inland were covered with salt spray. The *Liverpool Courier* called it "one of the most awful and destructive hurricanes that has occurred within the memory of the oldest inhabitant."

Prior to the storm's onset, outbound ships had been held up in port for days by a west wind. On Sunday, the 6th of January, the wind finally shifted direction, and a number of vessels—among them four packets bound for New York—set sail. That night, while the ships were still in the Mersey River, the wind shifted back to the west and strengthened, and by 2 o'clock the following morning it had reached hurricane force. On land, the *Courier* reported, "thousands of families arose from their beds, unable to rest, from the terror inspired by the roaring of the tempest." On the Mersey, the brutal wind snapped masts like matchsticks, ripped canvas to shreds and left ships bobbing like corks on the roiling waters. When daylight came, 15 vessels had gone aground.

The Black Ball packet *Oxford*—valued at $70,000—lay wrecked on the sand, all her masts down and her hull filling with water at high tide. Luckily, her passengers and crew got off safely, and so sturdy was her hull that she was soon back in service again. Her sister ship, the *Cambridge*, was even luckier—but only after a night's ordeal. Through two changes of tide she had been in danger of being dashed against a stone pier. Her captain hung a sign over the side of the ship, offering £1,000 to any steamship that would tow her out of harm's way. The offer had no takers. In the end, her dragging anchors held, and the ship was spared. The *Cambridge* sailed on the 10th of January, and was the first vessel to reach New York with news of the hurricane.

Much less fortunate than the two Black Ball liners were the 651-ton *St. Andrew* of the Red Star Line and the Blue Swallowtail's 808-ton *Pennsylvania*. When the hurricane struck in the small hours of Monday morning, it tore the *St. Andrew's* brand-new sails to ribbons. Her captain ordered the men aloft, but one of them had just been thrown from the yardarm to the deck and severely injured. With "death staring them in the face," the *Liverpool Albion* reported, the men refused the captain's order. The ship floundered, unmanageable, for hours. Finally some sails lower on the mast were rigged, and she struggled to return to Liverpool.

Around 10:30 on Tuesday morning, the *St. Andrew* struck a sandbar and lay there "with both anchors down," the newspaper said, "the sea beating heavily." The captain—being "apprehensive of the consequences to the crew"—ordered all liquor casks smashed and dumped over the side. At half past three that afternoon, the steam tugboat *Victoria*—sent by harbor authorities to help as many disabled ships as she could—came alongside. All 23 persons aboard the foundering *St. Andrew* were carried safely to the steamer in the ship's boats. But the *St. Andrew* was a total wreck.

The travail of the 40 persons aboard the *Pennsylvania* was even worse. Like the *St. Andrew*, the *Pennsylvania* also got stuck on a sandbar, but when one of her boats put off, with 11 people aboard, it swamped and drowned 10 of them. Twenty-nine crewmen remained on the sinking ship until Wednesday morning. When the *Victoria* found them, they were clinging to the rigging, reported the newspaper, "benumbed with cold, the sea having been washing over them all night and morning." Three crew members had died during the ordeal, and the captain and the second mate had been swept overboard and drowned. The *Victoria* rescued 25 people; 15 had perished. The $70,000 ship and her nearly one million dollars' worth of cargo were a complete loss.

A shipping calamity ashore

Of all the disasters that afflicted the American shipping industry during the 19th Century, none was so financially devastating as the fire that swept through New York City's business district during the night of December 16, 1835. In less than 24 hours, the conflagration destroyed 674 buildings —many of them the countinghouses and warehouses of merchants engaged in transatlantic trade.

The fire broke out shortly after 9 p.m., when a gas pipe exploded in a dry-goods warehouse. Although firemen reached the scene quickly, they were exhausted from having fought a large fire the night before. To make matters worse, temperatures had hovered below zero for more than a week, and hydrants were frozen solid. Water was obtained by cutting through the harbor ice, but it froze during its passage through the hoses, emerging with almost no pressure.

Whipped by high winds, the fire spread with horrifying rapidity. Soon clouds of smoke enveloped all of lower Manhattan, and the flames shot so high that their glow was visible up to 100 miles away.

Sailors fought frantically to protect their ships before the flames reached the docks. A quick-thinking shipmaster ran up and down the wharves, ordering seamen to get all sails belowdecks so they would not be ignited by airborne embers. Fortunately, the East River channel had been kept open, and many ships were able to escape destruction by moving out into open waters. Only a few vessels caught fire, and their crews managed to extinguish the flames themselves.

Ashore, however, the scene was one of total chaos. As warehouses were threatened by fire, their proprietors heaved entire shipments of lace, indigo, silk, tea and other valuable commodities into the street. One group of merchants, having heaped all their goods in a spot that they thought safely distant from their warehouse, watched aghast as the warehouse ignited and shot a great tongue of wind-blown flame straight to their merchandise, turning it into a fiery mountain.

Nor was the fire the only destroyer. Mobs roamed the city's streets, gathering up all the goods they could carry. During the nightlong saturnalia, members of the mob grew progressively more violent as they consumed thousands of bottles of looted liquor.

The next day, fire fighters finally managed to bring the conflagration under control by razing a number of buildings with gunpowder to create firebreaks. By that time, 52 acres of New York City's business district had been reduced to ruins. Only two people had perished, but many thousands were left jobless. So enormous were the insurance claims brought by the victims that most underwriters could not hope to pay them off: They simply closed their doors for good. Many of the merchants who had made fortunes in the packet trade had lost everything—everything, that is, except the ships that would enable them to make fortunes again.

The Atlantic had another, subtler way of making known its destructive power. Occasionally (but fortunately not often) the marine columns in newspapers would print the dread phrase "went missing" next to a vessel's name—meaning the ship had simply vanished on the high seas. There seemed to be no pattern to such incidents. Small vessels and large, eastbound and westbound—the ocean swallowed them without a trace. In the winter of 1826, a series of severe storms made for many slow crossings. By late March, no fewer than 13 packets were overdue in New York. During the first week of April, 12 of those ships arrived in port. The 336-ton *Crisis* was the unlucky 13th; she had been spotted twice by a British brig, the last time on March 18, when she had been nearing some ice fields, but no more was ever heard of her.

There were other bad winters in the next two decades, but no further disappearing acts until the 650-ton Red Star liner *United States* and the 729-ton Black Baller *England* left Liverpool within a week of each other in November 1844. The *England* carried no passengers, the other ship only one; both had crews of 25 to 30 men. Though both ships for the most part had made the crossing in good time in the past, no one in New York was much concerned when they were a bit late in arriving this trip: After

Preserved from calamity by the East River, residents of Brooklyn look on as flames erupt from Manhattan's business district.

all, the *England* had once taken 49 days for a westward passage, and the *United States* had a 54-day trip on her record. But as January passed with no sign of either vessel, alarm grew. In mid-February, another ship brought news of a tremendous gale that had left a London packet stripped of her spars and had nearly engulfed the strapping new packet *John R. Skiddy*. "Many of those who before had a hope," wrote the *New York Herald*, "have ceased to cling to it." But the *Herald* itself did not finally give the ships up for lost until March 7, when it reluctantly removed the names of the *England* and the *United States* from the list of "Packets to Arrive" and designated them as ships that "went missing."

Although storms claimed more packets than any other type of disaster, no shipboard hazard was more dreaded than fire. On a foundering vessel, the ship's boats offered hope of escape; but on a burning ship, passengers and crew were in double jeopardy, for the boats were as vulnerable to flames as the rest of the vessel. The worst ordeal of this type was suffered by the 1,301-ton *Ocean Monarch* on August 24, 1848.

That morning, the *Ocean Monarch*—the first of three ships to bear that name—set out on her fourth voyage from Liverpool to Boston. Her hold contained a varied cargo: iron, dry goods, salt, light merchandise and earthenware packed in crates stuffed with straw. Nearly 400 passengers were aboard, 322 of them emigrants in the steerage spaces.

Shortly after dawn, a steam tugboat towed the packet out into the Mersey on her way to open water at the estuary. At 8 a.m., the pilot and tug left the *Ocean Monarch* and the wind filled her sails. As the packet beat her way downchannel, she passed the 1,404-ton *New World*, the largest packet afloat, which was also sailing with a full complement of steerage passengers. "Many a time during the morning did we look out and view the *Ocean Monarch*," recalled the Reverend S. Remington, a passenger aboard the *New World*, "not only on account of her beauty and symmetry, but because of her even match for the *New World* and the kind of competition there was between the two noble ships as to the speed of each. Evidently there was to be a trial between them this voyage, to determine which of the two could beat."

But competition was soon foreclosed. Around noon, the *Ocean Monarch*'s steward told Captain James Murdock that there was a fire in a ventilator in the afterpart of the ship, started by a steerage passenger who had wanted to cook a meal. Later, however, a crewman testified that he had seen another sailor go down into the hold with a lighted candle and return without it. Whatever the exact cause, it fast became irrelevant. When the captain went below, he found the main cabin full of smoke. He ordered his men to throw water over the flames, but the fire was already raging hopelessly out of control. Within five minutes, all of the after section was ablaze. Captain Murdock returned to the deck and ordered the helmsman to turn the vessel into the wind—an attempt to slow the spread of the fire by blowing the flames over the stern. Panicked passengers were scrambling up from below and pushing forward to escape the flames, smoke and heat. "Yells and screams of the most horrifying description were uttered," Murdock later recounted. "My voice could not be heard, nor my orders obeyed."

Sturdy workhorse of the transatlantic shuttle

If any one factor exercised a dominant influence on the design of packets, it was adversity. These ships had to withstand not only the paroxysmal violence of the North Atlantic but also the endless strain imposed by captains bent on keeping to schedule no matter what the circumstances.

Despite differences in size, speed and cargo capacity, the packets as a group had a number of features in common. They were all full-rigged ships, with square sails on the foremast, mizzenmast and mainmast; and their stout hulls were about four times as long as they were wide. A typical packet of the 1840s—such as the one pictured below and on the following pages—measured about 1,000 tons, was 170 feet from stem to stern and had a hold 20 feet deep.

Timber from live oak, unsurpassed for its tough fibers and fine grain, made the packet's hull durable and virtually impervious to dry rot. Copper sheathing on the bottom prevented leakage and protected against marine parasites. For strength, the masts, towering as much as 90 feet above their footing on the keelson, were made from a single tree trunk. The only timber that possessed the necessary height and resilience was white pine, which was floated from Maine to the New York shipyards where most packets were built.

Though unarmed, the packet had painted-on gunports that gave it a threatening appearance. This masquerade dated to an earlier era when privateers prowled the sea; although no packet was ever attacked, the false gunports were retained as long as the transatlantic shuttle operated.

A real source of danger was the sea itself, and packets adapted in many ways, great and small. For example, instead of carrying an intricate figurehead, which might be damaged as the ship drove through stormy seas, the packet had a simpler billethead of wooden scrollwork. And as insurance against more serious damage, the packet carried extra spars and as many as three complete sets of sails. Some ships even kept a special set of winter sails made of duck cloth, heavy enough to stand up to a January gale.

A 1,000-TON PACKET OF THE 1840S

The packet was a transport ship par excellence, conveying goods and people across the ocean with unprecedented efficiency. Stowed in the hold on the eastbound passage were commodities such as cotton, grain and tobacco; westbound, the ship might carry crockery, textiles and coal. Above the hold, in a poorly ventilated, gloomy space known as steerage, or 'tween decks, the packet carried its most profitable cargo—emigrants heading for a new life in America. These passengers were jammed into rickety wooden berths fastened to the deck beams; on many ships they had to prepare their own meals, climbing a ladder to reach a galley stove on the main deck.

Cabin passengers, in contrast, lived in another world. Their two-person staterooms, with louvered doors for ventilation, were located aft on the main deck. They took their meals in a dining room brightened by a skylight and afterward could retire to a smoking compartment near the wheelhouse on the poop deck. The captain and officers occupied comfortable staterooms in the stern, while crewmen were berthed in deckhouse and forecastle quarters more comparable to steerage accommodations.

The better packets boasted some newfangled features intended to improve the quality of life. Instead of relying on chamber pots for sanitation, they had water closets—deck-level stalls with wooden seats opening out to the sea through the bulwarks. The old ships had stored the ship's drinking water in scores of old wine casks that soon turned their contents foul. The newer ones kept the water in two huge iron tanks located in the hold; the tanks fed water, by means of pipes and a pump, to the poop deck. Unfortunately, these innovations did not always work to the benefit of the hapless souls in steerage. In storms, the hatches were battened down, and the steerage passengers had to endure thirst and sanitary chaos until the weather cleared.

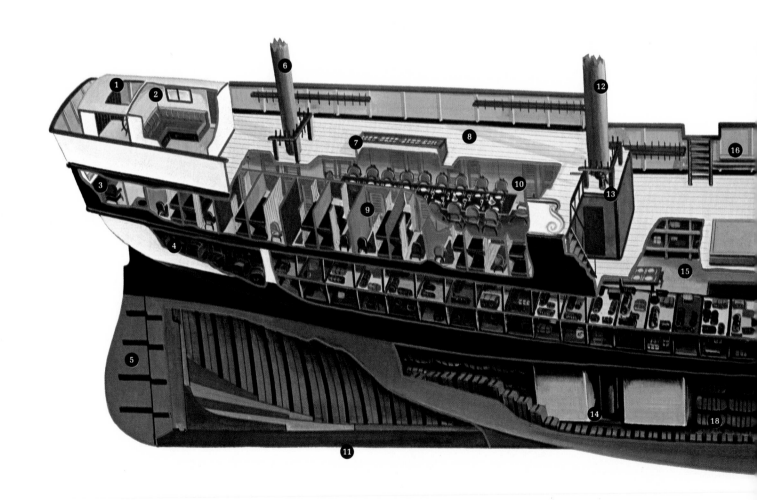

1. WHEELHOUSE
2. SMOKING COMPARTMENT
3. CAPTAIN'S CABIN
4. LUGGAGE COMPARTMENT
5. RUDDER
6. MIZZENMAST
7. SKYLIGHT
8. POOP DECK
9. STATEROOMS
10. DINING ROOM AND SALOON
11. KEEL
12. MAINMAST
13. WATER PUMP
14. IRON WATER TANKS
15. STEERAGE
16. SPARE SPARS

17. ANIMAL PENS
18. CARGO HOLD
19. SHIP'S BOAT
20. DECKHOUSE
21. GALLEY
22. GALLEY STOVE
23. BULWARK
24. COPPER SHEATHING
25. FOREMAST
26. WATER CLOSET
27. FORECASTLE CREW'S QUARTERS
28. WINDLASS
29. CAPSTAN
30. FORECASTLE DECK
31. BOWSPRIT
32. BILLETHEAD

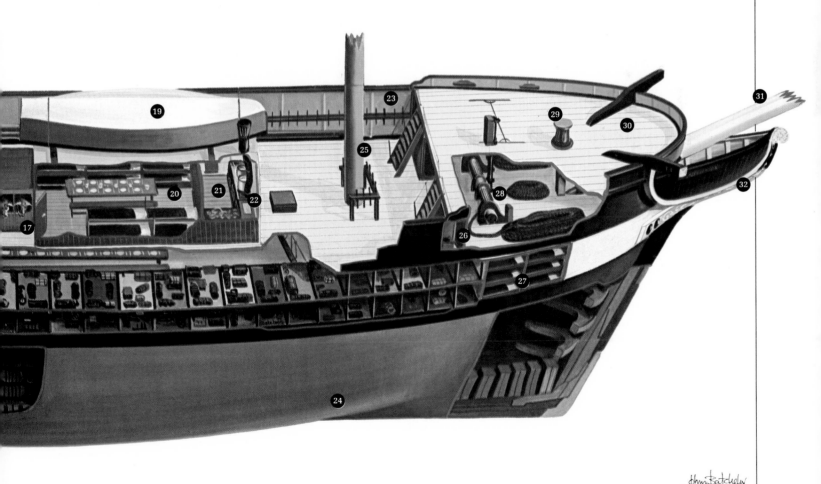

The scene on deck grew progressively more nightmarish. Men and women rushed back and forth trying to find husbands, wives and children. One eyewitness later recalled that "while some were standing in resignation, or insensibility, others were yielding to the most frantic despair. Several of the emigrants' wives and children were engaged in prayer and in reading the Scriptures." Murdock ordered the ship's boats lowered, and the crew succeeded in getting two into the water. The first mate, and some of the crew and passengers got away in these; the custom of women and children first was ignored. The other boats were destroyed by the fire before their lashings could be cut. Murdock, who was still on board, endeavored to throw a spare yard over the side so that those struggling in the water would have something to cling to. Then, almost trapped by flames, the captain jumped over the side himself.

Fortunately, the *Ocean Monarch* was still in the Mersey estuary, a waterway alive with incoming and outgoing ships. A passing yacht, the *Queen of the Ocean*, rescued Murdock after he had clung to a floating board for half an hour. The yacht belonged to Thomas Littledale, Commodore of the Royal Mersey Yacht Club. Littledale, who was returning from an outing with a party of friends, staunchly kept his vessel alongside the *Ocean Monarch* for two hours, saving as many lives as possible. A Brazilian steam frigate, the *Affonso*, was also coming into har-

As the packet Ocean Monarch burns in the Mersey estuary on August 24, 1848, passengers clamber onto the bowsprit to escape the flames. Many passengers jumped overboard and drowned.

bor when she sighted the burning ship. The *New World* and another outward-bound vessel, the *Prince of Wales*, turned around to give the stricken ship what assistance they could. Boats from all four vessels shuttled back and forth, picking up survivors in the water, taking them to safety and returning for a new load.

By late afternoon the fire had consumed so much of the *Ocean Monarch* that passengers sought refuge on the bowsprit and jib boom. From the deck of the *New World*, pastor Remington could see men and women packed tightly against and atop one another, "strung out like bunches of grapes." Then the foremast collapsed over the side, dragging with it much of the jib boom's rigging and the screaming people who were hanging on to it.

For more than an hour, a dozen or so women and children continued to cling desperately to the bowsprit, so immobilized by fear that they would not let go and drop into the water, even though rescuers waited below in boats. Finally, a seaman on the *New World*, Frederick Jerome, stripped off his clothing, swam under the bow of the burning *Ocean Monarch* and climbed up a rope that was hanging from the vessel. One by one he lowered the passengers to safety—although, as Remington reported, "the bowsprit was tottering to its fall, and the ship every moment expected to sink." The last passenger saved was an old man who had been sheltering a small child.

All that day and into the night the fire blazed, devouring the *Ocean Monarch* down to the water line. Then the sea reached over the edge of the ravaged hull, quenched the flames and, at about 1:15 Friday morning, sank what remained of what Remington had called one of the "finest and most magnificent ships afloat." The death toll was a staggering 178. Through their combined efforts, the *Queen of the Ocean* and the *Affonso* had rescued a total of 188 people. The other vessels had saved 30 more. All of the first-class passengers had escaped with their lives, as had a good part of the 42-man crew. But of the 322 passengers in steerage, fewer than 200 survived the disaster.

For his bravery, the 24-year-old Frederick Jerome was promptly given £20 in gold by a wealthy admirer aboard the *Affonso*. Later, the City of New York presented him with an inscribed gold box worth $150.

Fire did not always work so swiftly as on the *Ocean Monarch*. One packet that experienced its horrors in more protracted form was the *Poland*, eastbound from New York to Le Havre in May 1840, under the command of Captain Caleb Anthony Jr. Five days out of New York, a bolt of lightning struck the *Poland*'s foremast and traveled down to the lower hold, setting fire to some of the 270 bales of cotton that had been stowed there. The cotton lay beyond reach of the crew, under 2,700 barrels of flour, 22 barrels of potash and other cargo that made the hold a tinderbox. The sailors battened down the hatches in an effort to put out the fire by depriving it of air, but the cotton continued to burn. When Captain Anthony realized that the ship was lost, he ordered the vessel's boats lowered and loaded them with 32 of the 35 passengers, including all of the women and children. The boats were stocked with provisions and towed behind the burning vessel, which was moving slowly under a

Seaman Frederick Jerome risked his life by hanging from the bowsprit of the burning Ocean Monarch to hand the last of the passengers down to the safety of a lifeboat. When the City of New York presented him with a gold box for his bravery, he asked a minister to express his thanks to the assembled crowd.

light wind. The captain occasionally sent the passengers encouragement in the form of hot coffee and roast chicken. The remaining 37 voyagers spent the night on the steadily warming deck.

On the following day the wind rose, making the ride in the ship's boats extremely uncomfortable. Those passengers were then brought back aboard the *Poland*, and all sail was set in the hope of coming across another vessel. And so they did. At two in the afternoon, the New York-bound packet *Clifton* was sighted and the *Poland* headed toward her. The wind had turned into a gale and the seas were running high. With every pitch and roll, smoke streamed through the seams of the burning vessel. It took six hours of hard work for the ships' boats to transfer the *Poland's* passengers and crew to safety. At the end, with the fire in the hold ready to burst through the scorching deck at any moment, Captain Anthony abandoned his merciful plan to shoot the ship's cow. It was left—the only casualty—to burn with the ship.

The lack of an adequate number of boats on the *Poland* was all too typical of packets. In her case, extraordinary good luck prevented tragedy. But the very next year, a gruesome price was paid for the shortage of emergency craft on another ship in distress.

In June 1841, the *William Brown* was taking the northern route to Philadelphia when she collided with an iceberg. Her hull was so badly holed that there was no hope of saving the vessel. As she began to settle lower in the water, the instinct for survival overcame sentiments of duty and compassion. Crewmen launched the ship's boats, took on some passengers—enough to overburden the boats—and pulled away in a trice, leaving more than 30 people behind. As self-appointed commander of the longboat, Mate Alexander W. Holmes decided that his craft would sink unless its load of 33 people was reduced. Holmes therefore ordered the crewmen to throw 16 passengers overboard. Making no protest, the crew reached first for a man named Frank Carr. He tried to talk them out of it. "I'll work like a man till morning, and do what I can to keep the boat clear of water," he said. "I have five sovereigns and I'll give it for my life till morning, and when morning comes, if God does not help us, we will cast lots, and I'd go out like a man if it is my turn." But Carr's pleas were in vain; he was heaved over.

Then his youngest sister Mary cried out, "If you put him out, put me out too. I'm willing to die the death of my brother, but don't part me and my brother." The sailors took her at her word, threw her over the side and then jettisoned another sister. The boat, however, was rescued by a passing vessel not long afterward. In the federal court of Philadelphia some time later, Holmes was tried and convicted of manslaughter

From aboard two crowded longboats and the deck of their flaming ship, passengers and crewmen of the packet Poland sight merciful deliverance as another packet, the Clifton, emerges from a squall in the distance. Hit by lightning in midocean in 1840, the Poland burned for nearly two days before help arrived.

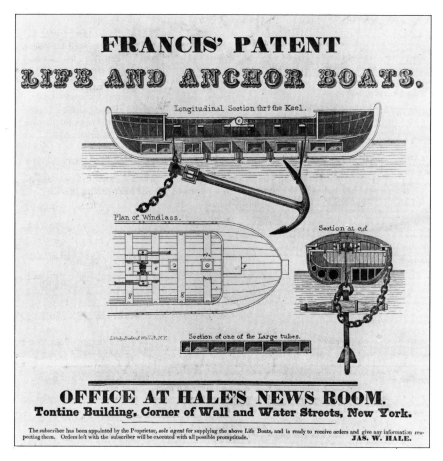

These illustrations accompanied an 1839 broadside advertising Joseph Francis' unsinkable wooden lifeboats. The honeycombed sections belowdecks were filled with hydrogen, giving the boat enough buoyancy to hold 300 persons, or a 2,000-pound anchor and a crew. The anchor, lowered and raised by means of the windlass amidships, could be used to dislodge another vessel's anchor from a rocky or muddy bottom.

on the heart-rending testimony of the few passengers he had allowed to remain in the longboat.

Not only did the packets carry too few boats, but the few that they did carry had not been designed to withstand the rough treatment they got in the frantic activity aboard a foundering ship. They were so flimsy that if the lines from the davits on which a boat was slung broke as the boat was lowered, the fall often smashed the boat's sides. Even if a boat and its passengers were successfully lowered, the craft was no match for raging seas or pounding surf. It was easily overturned, and if waves crested the gunwales, the boat swamped in moments. The longboat—the only ship's boat that could hold a significant number of people—had a special problem of its own. On passenger vessels, it generally served as the place to keep the cow that was carried to provide fresh milk during the voyage. Enough manure accumulated to ensure that the bottom of the boat would rot through in the course of a few trips.

The flaws of the ships' boats were widely known—and generally ignored. To shipowners and ship captains they were as much to be expected as salt in the sails. But to a Bostonian named Joseph Francis, these flaws were a challenge. In 1812, as an inventive 11-year-old, Francis had built a small, unsinkable boat using cork-filled buoyancy chambers in the bow and stern. Seven years later, he won a prize from the Massachusetts Mechanics' Institute for a rowboat that incorporated the same features. On the strength of this success, Francis moved to New York to seek backers or buyers for his unsinkable boats. His first years in New York were discouraging, but he continued to make improvements to his invention—and even found a few customers. In 1828, for example, he received contracts to build his unsinkable boats for the frigate *Santee* and the ship of the line *Alabama*.

In 1837, Francis staged an unforgettable demonstration of his latest-model lifeboat before a maritime audience in New York. In addition to the cork flotation compartments bow and stern, this stoutly built wooden boat had copper air chambers along the sides and under the thwarts. It was also equipped with looped life lines attached to the sides, so that 30 or 40 people could hang on to the boat if there was not enough room inside it. To prove its prowess, the boat was taken to the foot of Wall Street and thrown into the water end-first and upside down. "She instantly righted," said one report, "and freed herself of water which passed through the perforated bottom." Attempts were then made to sink the craft by pumping water into her "with the power of two fire engines, but it ran out of the holes in her bottom as fast as pumped in." Then, the report continued, a line was fixed to the boat and to the yard-arm of the brig *Madison*. The boat was hauled to the top of the yardarm and again dropped endwise into the water. Although it smacked the surface with considerable force, "she sunk only two feet into the water, and falling over, came to her right position." Finally, the boat was loaded with a number of men who—despite all efforts—"could neither upset or sink her."

After this demonstration and a similar one held in Philadelphia, Francis' future was secure. Orders for his revolutionary craft began to pour in from all over Europe as well as from the United States. In 1840, all U.S. men-of-war were required to carry Francis' Life-Boats. Tales of daring rescues in them accumulated. In one instance, a lifeboat was sent in heavy weather by the New York packet *Rhone*—en route from Le Havre—to save the crew of the sinking British bark *Bolinda;* the sea was so rough that the lifeboat had a hole smashed in its bottom as it was being lowered into the water—yet the boat was rowed more than a mile to fulfill its mission.

Inevitably, public pressure forced packet owners to purchase these craft, but not without resistance on the part of both owners and ship captains. The owners objected to the added expense of the newfangled boats, the captains to any mandatory cluttering up of their ships' quarter-decks—and to the imagined insults to their vessels' seaworthiness and their own seamanship. Some shipowners, venal and myopic to the end, ordered the smallest model made—one that was able to carry only five persons—but most took their passengers' safety to heart and outfitted their packets adequately.

Refusing to rest on his laurels, Francis continued to experiment. He concluded that he could build a better lifeboat with iron sheets, which had a greater strength-to-weight ratio than wood. After nearly a year of effort, Francis developed a press and dies that produced smoothly curved pieces of metal for the boat's sides. But to the inventor's intense disappointment, the metal would not hold its shape when removed from the dies. Francis threw away the faulty dies and began again. Eventually, he became convinced that if he could devise a method of corrugating the thin sheets of iron, he could retain the innate strength of the metal and also achieve the necessary stiffness. It took four years of difficult and costly work, but in 1845 Francis had perfected a process for making the lifeboat he envisioned.

In its final form, the process utilized two cast-iron dies weighing three tons apiece. When a sheet of iron was placed between them and hydraulic pressure applied, the finished sheet was deeply corrugated and held its shape. Two such sheets joined together made a complete boat, so strong that it needed no ribs or other internal bracings.

Over the years, these boats, like Francis' earlier ones, were subjected to dramatic tests. In one instance, a metal lifeboat was filled to the gunwales with paving stones, suspended more than 10 feet above a rocky surface, and then cut loose. "To the surprise of all who witnessed the experiment," said an observer, "she did not receive the least injury, as she was at once launched and rowed to the dock." Word of this astonishing durability spread, and by 1848 both American and British ships were carrying the metal lifeboats. Formal government recognition of the worth of Francis' invention came when the U.S. Congress passed the Steamboat Law of 1852 requiring every passenger vessel to carry at least one of these craft.

In the meantime, Francis moved on to his next dream—to make a boat that would be capable of saving the lives of people who were wrecked just offshore, where crashing breakers could destroy rescue boats launched from the beach as well as lifeboats lowered from the stranded vessel. Within two years of receiving the patent for the corrugated metal boat, Francis had constructed a contrivance he called a life car. This was an enclosed metal boat, capable of holding four or five persons, that could be hauled to and from a wreck on a heavy hawser. The complete system included a mortar—a small cannon that shot a lightweight line out to the wrecked ship. With this line, people on the ship could haul in both the hawser from which the life car would be suspended and another rope, which would be used—by means of a pulley system—to pull the car back and forth between ship and shore. On the shore, the ropes were attached to a post or to wooden stakes that were tall enough to raise the life car above the surf.

Francis' car got its first test on January 12, 1850, when a violent gale drove the packet *Ayrshire* ashore at Squam Beach, a particularly dangerous section of the New Jersey coastline. Rescuers on the shore set up the mortar, aimed it, and on the very first shot sent a line across the ship's deck. Moments later, the life car made the first of 60 trips through the surf; eventually 200 passengers and 47 crewmen were carried to safety. The only casualty was a passenger who drowned through his own fault. His family was already in the car, but there was no more room for him. Refusing to wait for the next trip, he clung to the outside of the car as it was dragged toward the shore—and he was swept off by a wave.

This spectacular rescue operation was made possible by another development that would be of the utmost importance to the packet trade and to all subsequent vessels crossing the Atlantic: the creation of an

This hydraulic press, designed by Joseph Francis, made possible the construction of metal lifeboats that were far stronger than his earlier, wooden versions. When workmen operated the pumps at left, a die rode upward on 800 tons of water pressure, forcing a galvanized sheet of iron against another die above and giving the sheet the rounded shape of half a boat.

With three passengers cramped under a hood (inset), a Joseph Francis Life-Car rides safely over violent surf by means of a cable strung from the grounded packet Ayrshire to the New Jersey beach. So spectacular was the life car's performance in this 1850 shipwreck that the U.S. government immediately ordered 30 more of the devices for distribution to lifesaving stations along the Atlantic coast.

organized system of coastal lifesaving stations. For centuries, mariners driven ashore in storms were likely to die in the bludgeoning seas before help came. Even if their plight was seen, people on shore did not always give them aid. In 1825 a ship captain registered the first of many complaints that the fishermen living along the New Jersey coast were more interested in looting than in saving lives. In April of that year, the coastal packet *Franklin* ran aground in heavy fog on a stretch of land called Island Beach. Not long after the grounding, a crowd appeared. "I thought we were cast upon a hospitable shore," the *Franklin*'s captain, John Munro, later reported. He was soon disabused of that notion. "Out of 200 or more who assembled on the beach," Munro wrote, all but 20 "plundered us for everything they could get hold of."

These New Jersey "pirates," as Munro called them, were still in evidence 21 years later, when another coastal packet, the *John Minturn*, was wrecked on Squam Beach in February of 1846. Again a crowd materialized on the beach and looted the ship's cargo as it washed ashore—ignoring the cries for help from the passengers and crewmen who clung to the icy rigging of the stranded vessel. Thirty-eight people froze to death, including the captain, his wife and their children.

But not all who lived near the sea were so lacking in compassion. In Massachusetts, for example, organized efforts to help shipwreck victims had begun as early as 1785, when the Massachusetts Humane Society—patterning itself after the British Royal Humane Society—built small shelters along the coast and stocked them with food, clothing and firewood for shipwreck survivors who might make their way there. In 1807, the society established the country's first lifeboat station at Cohasset on Massachusetts Bay, and by 1846 it was maintaining 18 stations and numerous "houses of refuge" along the Massachusetts coast.

Another locale with a long tradition of humanitarianism was the southern shore of Long Island. Veteran surfmen would launch a fishing dory at the first cry of "Ship ashore!" and village women would gather on the beach with food and warm clothing at the ready. But callousness was occasionally displayed even here—with predictably tragic results. On the night of January 1, 1837, for instance, the emigrant vessel *Mexico*, with 104 passengers aboard, arrived off Sandy Hook and hoisted signal lights for a pilot to guide her into New York harbor. There was no response. The pilot boats were snugly tied up at the pier, their occupants blithely celebrating the new year. After beating back and forth through the night and all the next day, the *Mexico* went aground off Hempstead, Long Island, in the midst of a storm. A small boat did manage to put out from shore—it took off the captain and seven crewmen, who landed and went on a futile search for help. All those still on board froze to death.

Following a series of such disasters, a group of concerned merchants, underwriters and shipowners formed the Life Saving Benevolent Association of New York in 1849. They financed the building of 10 lifesaving stations along the shores of Long Island, from Barren Island at the southeast entrance to New York harbor, to Amagansett, near the tip of Long Island, some 100 miles to the east.

Two years earlier, the federal government had belatedly acknowledged some responsibility for the safety of vessels approaching the nation's shores. In March 1847, Congress authorized the Secretary of the Treasury to apply $5,000 toward furnishing "the lighthouses on the Atlantic Coast with means of rendering assistance to shipwrecked mariners." But the government's good intentions went somewhat awry—as they would continue to do for nearly 30 years. In this instance, the money found its way into the hands of the collector of customs of Boston, where it was used by the Massachusetts Humane Society to build new lifeboat stations on the Massachusetts coast—a worthy enough endeavor, but not the intention of Congress.

The following year, a larger appropriation was made and its expenditure more carefully monitored—thanks to a freshman congressman from New Jersey. William A. Newell had been so horrified by the sight of bodies floating ashore after a shipwreck at Barnegat Inlet that the first measure he introduced upon being elected to Congress in 1848 was a bill to apply federal funds to the building of lifesaving stations. At his urging, Congress appropriated $10,000 to build some stations on a hazardous stretch of the New Jersey coast between Sandy Hook and Little Egg Harbor. It was this appropriation—expanded the next year and renewed each year thereafter—that enabled Joseph Francis' life cars to be used in the wreck of the *Ayrshire*. The stations, stated the appropriations bill, were to be equipped with surfboats, rockets and other equipment "for the better protection of life and property from shipwrecks." The Treasury Department was made responsible for their upkeep.

Within six years, 137 federally funded lifesaving stations had been established along U.S. seacoasts and the shores of the Great Lakes. Many of the pioneering private stations in Massachusetts and New York were gradually incorporated into the new federal system.

The increase in the number of stations significantly reduced the toll of deaths from shipwrecks—but the system was still far from perfect, for it depended completely on volunteers. The surfmen who manned the equipment had learned their skills in the course of their daily work, rowing their small wooden boats across the surf either to fish or to salvage flotsam. Their sole reward for risking their own lives to save others was the right to make a salvage deal with the insurance companies that held the policies on the shipwrecked vessels—not much of an incentive in brutal weather. In August of 1850, a volunteer lifesaver named Benjamin Downing spotted two men clinging to a schooner overturned in a storm near Eaton's Neck, New York. Downing, who was 66 years old, one-armed and lame, hauled a lifeboat to the water's edge with the help of two yoke of oxen. The lifeboat was 25 feet long and required six oarsmen. Six other volunteers were present, but they refused to man the boat because of the fierceness of the storm. Downing then recruited his 16-year-old son to help him, and together they took the boat out. They succeeded in saving one of the men on the schooner, but the other had tried to swim ashore and was drowned. Though Downing and his son were rewarded for their extraordinary performance, no action could be taken against the reluctant volunteers.

Another dubious assumption of those who made the first attempts to establish a lifesaving system was that volunteers would reach the scene of a shipwreck quickly. But volunteers did not live at the stations. When a wreck was spotted, word was sent around by any available means. The volunteers all had to make their way to the station where the equipment was kept, and then drag the life car and the mortar to the site of the wreck itself—which might well be several miles away over rough terrain. High winds, snow and darkness would naturally add to the delays.

Just how ineffective this system could be was demonstrated at Long Beach, New Jersey, in April 1854. Flung ashore during the night by a raging northeaster, the emigrant vessel *Powhatan*, carrying 250 passengers and crew, shuddered to a halt barely eight yards from the low-water mark. The vessel was so tantalizingly near to safety that, after dawn, passengers and crew carried on a shouted exchange with people on the beach. To despairing pleas for help, the watchers replied that the lifesaving crew had been summoned during the night and should be arriving at any moment. But the hours passed with no sign of them. Huge waves washed over the deck, flicking passengers off into the raging surf. The voice of the captain could be heard begging the watchers, "For God's sake, save some of those who are drowning!" It was an impossible hope. At dusk, an enormous wave struck the battered ship. One section of the bulwarks collapsed, carrying with it dozens of passengers. Then the entire hull crumbled. The beach was littered with bodies, personal effects and freight. No one survived.

A day and a half after the *Powhatan* was grounded, the crew from the nearest lifesaving station—six miles away—finally arrived. On the night of the wreck, they had set forth, dragging their life car and mortar.

WARNING A VESSEL
AWAY FROM SHORE.

DRAGGING LIFE-BOAT
TO THE BEACH.

LAUNCHING
LIFE-BOAT.

THE GUN CART.

SIGNALLING
TO A VESSEL.

SIGNALLING AT NIGHT.

RESCUE WITH
BUOY AND HAWSER.

FIRING A LINE.

BEACHING
THE LIFE-BOAT.

A montage of sketches from an 1888 article on the Sandy Hook Lifesaving Station shows shore patrolmen in action at the southern entrance to New York harbor. The men who performed this work were old hands at coping with stormy waters; most had served as seamen aboard merchantmen and whalers before retiring to a life ashore.

But the storm had been so fierce that two of the rescue workers had collapsed from exhaustion and had to be helped back to the shelter of the station by the others. There they huddled until the storm subsided.

The *Powhatan* disaster spurred Congress to action. Before the year was out, the Secretary of the Treasury was authorized to release funds for more lifesaving stations, thus lessening the distance between them. The Secretary was also instructed to appoint "keepers"—at $200 a year— who would live at or near their assigned stations, where they could be easily found and could coordinate efforts to round up the other volunteers. This was an improvement, but there continued to be long, often fatal delays—in part because political favoritism infected the system.

The truth about this infection became known after the winter of 1870- 1871, when a number of terrible shipwrecks and the resulting loss of life prompted an investigation by the *New York Herald*. Some of the keepers, it turned out, lived anywhere from six to 100 miles away from their stations; often their only qualification for the job was having a good friend in Washington. This situation inevitably sapped morale. The *Herald* reported that crews rarely drilled in the use of their equipment, or felt any need to make regular patrols of their section of coastline.

The revelations brought an instant response: Congress appropriated $200,000 to improve the shaky organization of the lifesaving stations. At the same time, Sumner I. Kimball, Chief Clerk of the Treasury Department, was appointed head of the department's Revenue Marine Bureau and charged with making the necessary improvements.

Kimball wasted no time. He fired incompetent appointees and thoroughly reorganized the volunteer system into a professional service. Each lifeboat station now was staffed by a keeper—with the rank of boatswain—and six surfmen. All were paid, experienced men. Kimball assigned officers from the Treasury Department to supervise the overhaul of the stations and to train the crews in their new duties. The officers also instituted regular patrols of the section of the coast that each crew protected, bought new equipment for the stations and drew up standard regulations for the entire system. Control of the service remained centralized in Washington, D.C., but 12 district superintendents administered the regulations in their areas.

The reforms were so effective that in the first year of his supervision, Kimball could report that not one life was lost to shipwreck in any area where a lifesaving crew was within reach. In 1878, Kimball was named head of the United States Life Saving Service when it was reorganized as a separate bureau under the Treasury Department, and he stayed in that position until the service was merged with the Revenue Cutter Service to become the United States Coast Guard in 1915.

Kimball's reforms had come during the twilight years of the packet trade. By then, hundreds of packet passengers and crewmen had lost their lives, and cargo worth many millions of dollars had been lost. But not for a minute had the basic notion of packet service been called into question by shipowners or the public. So numerous were the benefits of the transocean shuttle that, despite the ever-present threat of tragedy, the Atlantic never came close to defeating the hardy breed of ships and men that first dared cross its expanse in all seasons and weather.

From Sandy Hook to dockside

No matter how many perils a packet eluded on her 3,000-mile passage, she faced one final challenge getting into port on either side of the Atlantic. Nowhere was the challenge stiffer than in New York. The entrance to New York harbor, a 25-mile stretch from Sandy Hook on the coast of New Jersey to the East River piers where the ships tied up, was an obstacle course of shifting shoals and strong currents that could ground a ship in a trice. Congestion, bred in part by the success of the packet lines, compounded the problems.

The best precaution against trouble in the closing phase of the journey was for the captain to take on board a harbor pilot—one of a talented breed of men who might never set sail on the high seas, but who knew the channels of the harbor like the veins on the backs of their hands, possessed an uncanny sensitivity to the caprices of the currents and winds, and could spot a shift in the lay of the undersea land by the subtlest change in the color of the water. The pilot's knowledge may have seemed arcane to the uninitiated, but his judgment received ample validation in the maritime industry. By 1837 the port of New York imposed a fine on any ship's captain foolhardy enough to venture into the harbor entrance without the aid of a pilot.

Procuring one was easy enough. As soon as a packet came within sight of the Sandy Hook Lightship, the captain simply sent up signal flares. As many as 18 pilot schooners were apt to be cruising the shore, and at the sight of the flares at least three or four were certain to race one another to the incoming ship. The packet captain usually gave the job to the winner, since all pilots charged a standard fee: The cost would range from about $25 to about $55, depending on the ship's size.

Once the pilot came aboard, the packet began a slow crawl into the harbor. The pilot himself was in no hurry—his reputation hung on his safety record, not on speed—and the port of New York required a pause for health inspection. If the packet passed inspection and the wind did not fail, she would arrive within 24 hours after picking up the pilot, but many a trip from Sandy Hook to dock stretched into days or even weeks.

On the poop deck of a packet nearing the Sandy Hook Lightship, the first mate uses a speaking trumpet to shout instructions to the men aloft, while the captain, beside him, watches a schooner launch a skiff that will bring over the harbor pilot. Two New York reporters have reached the ship first; at the hatch, one interviews passengers for news of the trip while another clutches an armload of English newspapers to take ashore. On the main deck beyond, other passengers strain for their first glimpse of America. The sight "compensates for all our toil and trouble," one steerage passenger wrote at the end of a crossing in 1848.

138

The harbor pilot reaches for the packet's rope ladder as a sailor hauls up his carpetbag. A pilot usually brought aboard a change of clothes for himself, and the latest New York newspapers for the captain and the cabin passengers.

While the captain stands by with a spyglass, the pilot points out a course that will take the ship past the Sandy Hook Lightship. The pilot did not assume command of the ship; he imparted the benefit of his wisdom to the captain, who then instructed the helmsman and mates.

Tied to the port-side rigging of the foremast, a sailor prepares to pitch a lead line and measure the depth of the channel. This operation—duplicated on the starboard side by another seaman —was performed continuously as the ship proceeded upchannel; the bottom might change configuration after a severe storm.

As the packet lies to off Staten Island, a watership pulls up to her starboard side to pump fresh water through the main hatch. Meanwhile, a skiff bearing a health inspector approaches her port side. If an inspector found cases of smallpox, cholera or typhus aboard, the sick would be hospitalized, and the ship might be quarantined for up to 30 days.

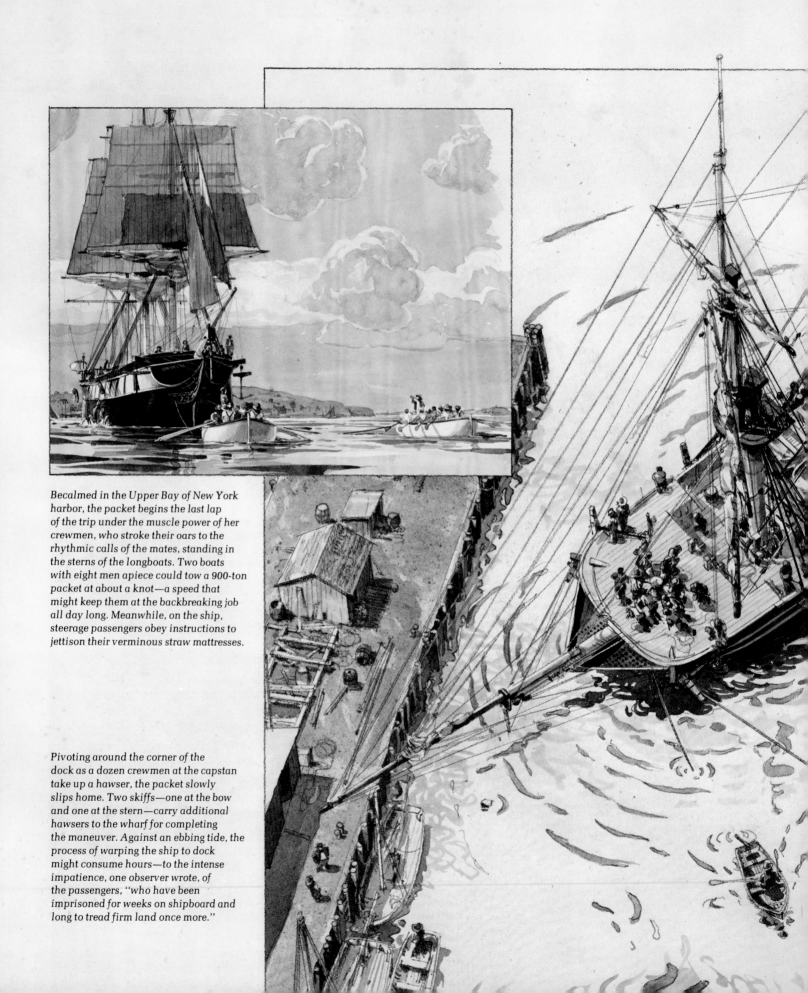

Becalmed in the Upper Bay of New York harbor, the packet begins the last lap of the trip under the muscle power of her crewmen, who stroke their oars to the rhythmic calls of the mates, standing in the sterns of the longboats. Two boats with eight men apiece could tow a 900-ton packet at about a knot—a speed that might keep them at the backbreaking job all day long. Meanwhile, on the ship, steerage passengers obey instructions to jettison their verminous straw mattresses.

Pivoting around the corner of the dock as a dozen crewmen at the capstan take up a hawser, the packet slowly slips home. Two skiffs—one at the bow and one at the stern—carry additional hawsers to the wharf for completing the maneuver. Against an ebbing tide, the process of warping the ship to dock might consume hours—to the intense impatience, one observer wrote, of the passengers, "who have been imprisoned for weeks on shipboard and long to tread firm land once more."

Chapter 5

Emigration at full tide

Elbow to elbow on the forecastle of a sailing packet, travelers bound for the United States wave to well-wishers as a steam tug pulls the vessel away from a Liverpool dock. Transatlantic packet traffic peaked in the 1850s; almost 1,000 crossings were made from the British Isles to North America in 1853 alone.

hick as flies upon a honey pot, they might be seen clambering over the side of the vessel, threading their difficult way among the ropes and cordage," wrote a journalist as he watched passengers crowding aboard a packet in Liverpool in 1850. Most of them, dressed in rags and booked for steerage quarters, were "pulled in any side or end foremost, like so many bundles," reported a passenger in the same year. A few, well-clothed and bound for cabin quarters, strolled up the gangplank with assurance, directing porters who carried their baggage for them.

All over the waterfront, an air of hectic festivity prevailed. Peddlers of ribbons and laces, oranges, candy and pocket mirrors swarmed through a confusion of cargo crates, water casks, miscellaneous baggage, departing voyagers and well-wishers. The sound of flutes, fiddles and bagpipes mingled with the wails of children and the chanteys of sailors. When a packet finally pulled out into the Mersey River, "the spectators on shore took off their hats and cheered lustily," and the people on deck answered with a shout that "must have been heard at the distance of a mile," the journalist wrote, "for hope was before them, and nothing was behind them but the remembrance of misery."

At the time, the migration that had begun with the Pilgrims more than two centuries before was reaching flood tide. Between 1846 and 1855, more than two million people sailed westward across the Atlantic— nearly half again as many as had made the journey in the seven decades between American independence and 1845. The great majority of the travelers were poverty-stricken and disenfranchised wretches fleeing political upheaval and repeated famine. But some among the wayfarers considered themselves "colonists" as opposed to mere "emigrants"— military men on half pay, for example, out to establish estates in the prospering New World and able to get there via the comfortable cabins that packet ships now afforded. And in their midst were businessmen, tourists and other affluent travelers who planned a round trip. All together, their patronage made the packet ship—as she shuttled back and forth across the Atlantic with the cargoes that sustained the commerce of both shores—the busiest ship on the seven seas.

For most of the passengers that the Liverpool journalist watched embark in such festive mood in 1850, the sea journey was to be a grim ordeal. That was nothing new, of course. Crossing the Atlantic had been a travail for emigrants ever since the earliest days of American settlement. In the 1840s, however, impoverished families crowded onto packets in such numbers that the old hazards of malnutrition and disease acted with especially horrific efficiency. Conditions aboard the ships would not improve appreciably until after the midpoint of the century, when packets began to lose customers to steamers and the desperate exodus from the Old World slackened a bit. Even then—indeed, for as long as packets bore a part of the emigrant traffic—many a passage would be a journey into nightmare.

The trip took 35 to 40 days on average, but perhaps twice that long if the ship met bad weather. Steerage passengers—typically as many as 800 of them on a 1,000-ton ship—would spend most of this time in the confines of a dark, rank, claustrophobic space known as between decks

("'tween decks" to seamen) that measured perhaps 100 feet by 25 or 30 feet. More often than not, the area was a makeshift adaptation to the growth of emigrant traffic; shipowners accommodated the new source of profit by building a flimsy, temporary floor beneath the main deck and on top of the cargo hold. Sometimes this flooring was set so far down in the hold that bilge water would seep up through the planking. Rats scurried about everywhere. Ventilation came only from the hatches, and these few sources of fresh air were closed tight during inclement weather. If there were portholes—an uncommon feature of such ships—they were set so low that they were awash at sea, could not be opened and were almost useless for illumination. The only light came from a few hanging lamps.

Into the 'tween decks were fitted row upon row of berths, about six feet long and set close together, in at least two tiers. Some ships were fitted out with three tiers of bunks; because the headroom in the 'tween decks was about five and a half feet, this arrangement left only about 25 inches between tiers, not enough for a person to sit up in his bunk. On many ships, the berths were no more than a foot and a half wide; on others they were six-by-six-foot squares designed to hold four persons—but usually crammed with more.

A sudden lurch of the ship as the wind gusted would sometimes topple the rickety bunks or catapult dozens of passengers out of their

To weed out anyone who slipped aboard without paying, a packet-line clerk stands on the forecastle rail and calls the roll for steerage passengers before departure; those who have been accounted for pass down the steps to the 'tween decks under the gaze of two crewmen. Some clerks jollied the crowd during this ritual by singing out impromptu couplets such as "William Jones, show your bones."

berths—children crying, men cursing, women screaming—to thrash about with baggage, food and flying slops buckets in what one steerage traveler called "a scene of misery and confusion such as I never saw before." During a storm, the misery was compounded by lack of access to the main deck. The hatches might be battened down for a week or more at a time—but not until after a few seas had poured in and soaked bedding and clothing alike. These would remain damp and reeking for the duration of the voyage.

From time to time, a probing finger of curiosity exposed the emigrants' conditions to the public. In 1847, an Irish landlord named Stephen de Vere—who happened to have an uncle in the House of Lords—crossed to America in steerage in order to observe firsthand the conditions of the voyage that so many of his former tenants were taking. He was appalled at what he found, and recorded his horror in a letter to his uncle: "Hundreds of poor people, men, women and children of all ages, from the drivelling idiot of ninety to the babe just born, huddled together without light, without air, wallowing in filth and breathing a fetid atmosphere, sick in body, dispirited in heart."

De Vere's detailed account, presented to a Parliamentary committee, aroused so much indignation that it resulted in the Passenger Vessel Act of 1848. Among other things, the Act specified that each passenger was entitled to space measuring six feet in height, two feet in width and a bit more than six feet in length. This worked out to 80 cubic feet—the amount of space that two tons of cargo would take up. As far as the shipowners were concerned, such a sacrifice of profit was simply unacceptable, and they chose to ignore the Act.

For a fee of three pounds five shillings—almost half a year's wages for many an Irish tenant farmer—this 1851 steerage ticket offers passage from Liverpool to New York aboard the packet ship Princeton. The contract promises food, water, cooking space aboard ship—and "subsistence money" of a shilling per person per day in the event the ship fails to depart Liverpool on schedule.

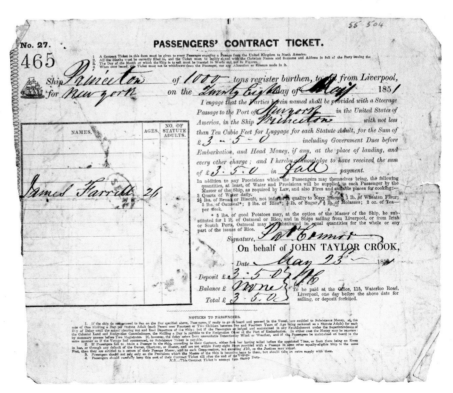

In truth, Parliament was reluctant to interfere with commercial trade—as was the United States Congress, which periodically enacted similar legislation on the opposite side of the Atlantic. Even in ports that had inspectors, ships might pass inspection, then pick up additional passengers from tenders when out of sight of the harbor. Sometimes there was no need for such subterfuge. Liverpool, the busiest emigration port of all, had only three inspectors. When favorable winds came up, as many as 30 ships might leave on the same tide from docks three miles apart; inspecting them all was patently impossible.

Most of the emigrant ships did not even provide for separation of the sexes. Unmarried men and women found themselves sharing the same four-person berths, often with married couples. A ship's mate, when questioned as to how connubial relations could take place in the absence of privacy, replied, "There is no difficulty as to that; there is plenty of that work going on every night to keep them in countenance." Perhaps so, but for many, the forced mingling of the sexes was a nightmare; in 1851 a minister testified before an investigative committee of Parliament that women sometimes sat up all night long on boxes rather than accept the alternative of sleeping under the same blanket with a strange man. Such testimony helped to spur the enactment the following year of another Passenger Vessel Act, this one stipulating that single men had to be berthed together in a separate section of steerage. Once again, however, captains and shipowners simply disregarded the Act.

Inevitably, the crowding bred stench and filth. When a government inspector in Canada examined the packet *Lady Macnaughton* upon her arrival in port, he reported that the few vacant spaces in the between decks were "filled with broken biscuit, bones, rags and refuse of every description, putrefying and filled with maggots."

Almost worse than the dirt was the smell. Some of the odors were those of a normal ship—the bilge and the perpetually rotting hulk, the lingering odor of old cargoes and foul new ones (such as hides). Herman Melville, who spent some time as a crewman on a transatlantic ship, recalled that, within a week of setting out, "to hold your head down the fore hatchway was like holding it down a suddenly opened cesspool."

When there were toilets—by no means a standard amenity—they were generally up on deck, beyond the reach of the more weakened passengers; in stormy weather, they were out of reach of everyone. The more usual facility in the 'tween decks consisted of a few screened-in buckets, which might or might not have seats. When seasickness struck, the buckets were so besieged that many passengers vomited in their berths. Water for washing was almost never available—and, in any case, washing was sometimes forbidden for fear that dampness would weaken the flimsy flooring.

Not only were steerage passengers subjected to the pernicious effects of overcrowding and filth, they were forced to subsist for weeks and months on a diet that, as one candid shipowner said, "is sufficient to stave off starvation, but is not enough to live upon and fructify." A witness who testified before a Parliamentary committee in 1844 described the dietary plight of these passengers in even grimmer terms:

Two engravings from the Illustrated
London News compare different
sorts of steerage accommodations. The
worst ships (top) crowded as many
as eight persons into a bunk. The better
ships (bottom) provided their passengers
the luxury of benches and tables.

"Their health suffered so much that their strength was gone, and they had not the power to help themselves." Statistics tell the tale: On some ships 10 per cent of the emigrants died at sea, and in bad years the average climbed to 16 per cent. The survivors were likely to come ashore suffering from malnutrition.

In the early years of the transatlantic migration, steerage passengers were expected to take with them virtually all the food that they would require during the voyage. Later, minimum provisions were mandated by British law, but they were so scanty as to jeopardize health. Every packet ship was supposed to provide each adult steerage passenger with a weekly allowance of two and a half pounds of biscuit, a pound of flour, five pounds of oatmeal, two pounds of rice, two ounces of tea, half a pound of sugar and half a pound of molasses; five pounds of potatoes could be substituted for one pound of oatmeal or rice. One doctor, asked if such an allowance was adequate, replied, "I do not think it is; I know it is not what you would give your servants." Meat and green vegetables were not included on the list of required provisions until 1848.

Predictably, shipowners and captains colluded to evade even these minimal dietary requirements. Under the watchful eye of port authorities, some captains would take on the stipulated amount of food, only to send it back later by tender and pocket the savings. If they did keep the food aboard, they would often sell it at extortionate prices to their passengers instead of distributing it free, as they were required to do by law.

A myriad of guidebooks—some well-intentioned, most impractical, and many selling thousands of copies during the peak emigration years—attempted to instruct the innocent emigrant in what food would be needed for the journey. One warned that the food provided by some shipmasters "is scarcely fit for hogs." Another suggested bringing 20 pounds of bacon, 50 pounds of fish and 672 pounds of potatoes, plus assorted other foodstuffs, as provisions for five for a journey of 60 to 70 days. Even if there had been room on board to store such a quantity of food it would have cost far more than the three pounds five shillings that the emigrants paid for their passage, a price they could scarcely afford.

For the emigrant, securing a life-sustaining supply of food was only half the battle; the other half was in trying to cook it. On most ships, the cooking grates up on deck were too few for the hundreds of people who needed to use them. When the weather was bad, the grates could not be used at all. Frederick Marshall, a Liverpool citizen who converted a waterfront warehouse into a boardinghouse for emigrants awaiting a ship's departure, made a crossing once himself, presumably to find out how his customers fared when they left him. His findings were thoroughly depressing. The ship he took had 400 passengers. Only six at a time could cook at the grates, and from dawn to dusk there was constant fighting for the privilege. Marshall observed that single women in particular had little chance of winning this struggle and many simply went hungry much of the time.

A traveler on another vessel reported that the ship's cooks did the cooking for steerage passengers—at a price. Those who could bribe the cooks with whiskey or money could have five hot meals a day. Those without the wherewithal had one meal a day—or one every other day.

A cartoon broadside published in 1833 satirizes America as a wilderness brimming with snakes, alligators, hostile Indians and other horrors, and ends by advising the unsuccessful settler to "work your passage back." Many disappointed emigrants did in fact go back; more than 18,000 left the New World for Liverpool in the year 1855 alone.

Equally scanty was the supply of drinking water. According to British law, every adult passenger was entitled to three quarts of fresh water daily. But many ships took on their water from the rivers in which they anchored, so it was not fresh to begin with. The law also specified that the water should be stored in "sweet casks"—that is, casks not befouled by having formerly held such contents as wine, indigo or tobacco. But many shipmasters used whatever containers they happened to have on hand, and even if the water was pure when taken on, it had generally turned rancid by the time it was issued. A passenger aboard a ship that stored its water in wine casks remembered it as "foul, muddy and bitter," adding that "the contents, when pumped out, resembled nauseous ditch water." Another received a ration that was "no clearer than that of a dirty kennel after a heavy shower of rain." The most common remedy for fouled water was to add vinegar; its acidity helped to check putrefaction but it did little to improve the taste and in the end only aggravated thirst.

The crews of some of the packets, far from sympathizing with the lot of the steerage passengers, added to their woes. The sailors sometimes forced their attentions upon female passengers and often stole the travelers' meager possessions. "Ours is one of the worst trades

Seated by his stove, a ship's cook glowers at steerage passengers clamoring for a meal. Though the tickets of the emigrants promised fixed rations of such basics as cereal, tea and water, some cooks demanded bribes for what they doled out.

in the world for seamen," said a man who spent much of his life in the emigrant business as a passenger broker in Liverpool. "In fact, we get a class of men who go more to pilfer from steerage passengers than for the purpose of going to sea."

Liquor flowed freely on most of the ships—"because it is profitable to the captain, who traffics in the grog," wrote an observer—and in a crew already inclined toward surliness, drink often spurred outright sadism. On one packet, abusive crew members directed fire hoses on the passengers just as the ship entered the St. Lawrence River in chilly midautumn. On another vessel, a collection of German, Swedish and Dutch passengers in steerage were pressed into work gangs, and, driven with ropes' ends, were made to do the crew's job of manning pumps.

The 1,655-ton Black Star ship *Washington* earned a particularly bad name for ill-treatment of her steerage passengers in 1851, as the result of a blistering report by a prominent Irish philanthropist named Vere Foster, who sailed aboard her in cabin class but busied himself with a close look at his less fortunate shipmates in steerage. The first of a number of incidents he noted took place almost as soon as the ship was under way. The 900 people in steerage were ordered to appear on deck for their water—all at the same time. Inevitably, a crush ensued, and the mates, in anger and frustration, struck and cursed them. In the scuffle, only about 30 of the passengers managed to fill their water cans.

For the next five days, the mates refused to give out any more rations, leaving those who had brought along no food of their own to go hungry. Foster took it upon himself to ask when the passengers would be fed. For his pains, he was punched in the face and knocked flat by the first mate.

On the sixth day, Foster protested to the captain, only to be threatened with being put in chains if he interfered further. But provisions finally were distributed, and Foster measured them with a scale that he had brought along for the purpose. He found that the passengers had received only half rations of biscuit and tea, short measures of oatmeal, molasses and rice, and none of the rations of vinegar and pork that had been promised with the fare.

These misfortunes were to be followed by another. Dysentery broke out among the emigrants, and the ship's doctor refused to venture down into the steerage to visit the sick. If they wanted medicine, he declared, "they must come to me." One of the passengers, himself a physician, attempted to collect donations for a gift to gain the doctor's favor. But none of the other passengers were willing to contribute, although some facetiously said that they would have no objection to giving a shilling to purchase a rope that could be used to hang the ship's surgeon.

Few ship's doctors were as negligent as the surgeon on the *Washington*. But even the most compassionate of physicians was helpless when disease struck the emigrants in steerage. Three diseases in particular were rampant on these ships: cholera, smallpox and typhus. Their prevalence was such that one captain was moved to write: "It is a wonder that so many survived the voyage as really did."

Theoretically, no emigrant was allowed to board a ship without having undergone a medical examination by a government doctor. But the examination was cursory, when it was made at all. One emigrant, describing his experience with a government doctor, reported: "I passed before him for inspection. He said, without drawing breath, 'What's your name? Are you well? Hold out your tongue; all right,' and then addressed himself to the next person." The doctors were paid one pound for every 100 persons they examined; an emigration officer in London testified that the government doctors inspected about 200 persons per hour—thus earning a very tidy income by the standards of the day.

Cholera, an infection of the stomach and intestines, was a particular problem on emigrant ships, for periodic epidemics swept through the British Isles. A ship that was stricken with cholera was helpless, since no one knew what to do about the disease. One recommended treatment was to administer a dose of Epsom salts and castor oil in combination, rub the patient's face with vinegar (presumably as a bracing astringent) and then give the patient 35 drops of laudanum—a highly addictive opiate. In practice, the ship's doctor might try anything he had in his medicine chest—which was apt to carry such dubious remedies as calomel, cream of tartar, peppermint, powdered rhubarb and some pills advertised on the waterfront as useful for curing 36 ailments.

Once cholera struck, it spread like wildfire. When the packet *Brutus* left Liverpool for the crossing in 1832, the disease was already incubating among the 330 steerage passengers who had boarded. Nine days after the ship set sail, the first case broke out; soon it was all over the *Brutus*. Twenty-four passengers died in a single day. When members of the crew came down with it, the captain decided to turn back. By the time the *Brutus* reached port 10 days later, 83 persons had died of the disease, and the remaining 200-odd passengers and crew carried it back into crowded Liverpool, where it spread further.

Most captains, instead of turning back, kept on going—and carried numbers of their passengers to certain death. When a cholera epidemic struck the transatlantic ships again in 1853, no fewer than 47 of the 312 vessels that arrived in New York during one four-month period had the disease on board—and 1,993 of their 96,000 passengers had been buried at sea.

Outbreaks of smallpox were less common but even more feared; the disease was often accompanied by pneumonia, encephalitis, blood poisoning or some other ailment, and the mortality rate was as high as 90 per cent. A cabin passenger who made the Atlantic crossing in 1845 wrote that when a man in steerage informed the ship's captain that there was smallpox on board, the shipmaster—who had just put on a brave display of "firm nerves" in a storm—"quailed at the hideous name of this scourge of God."

The worst killer of all on sailing ships was typhus—a liceborne disease that afflicts the victim's skin and brain, causing dizziness, headaches, and pain throughout the body, together with bloodshot eyes, a dark red rash and a dull, seemingly drunken stare. Typhus was so common in crowded conditions that it had been known for centuries by such names as "jail fever" and "camp fever." But when emigration by sailing ship was at its height, the disease inevitably acquired the name of "ship fever." It struck the packets with particular fury in 1847,

This warning notice, posted in government emigration offices in Liverpool after a serious cholera outbreak in 1853, urges travelers to dress warmly and eat well as precautions against the disease. The real cause of cholera, not known then, was contact with human waste—an inescapable hazard on overcrowded emigrant ships, where steerage passengers used common chamber pots that sometimes went unemptied for days.

TO EMIGRANTS.

CHOLERA.

CHOLERA having made its appearance on board several Passenger Ships proceeding from the United Kingdom to the United States of America, and having, in some instances, been very fatal, Her Majesty's Colonial Land and Emigration Commissioners feel it their duty to recommend to the Parents of Families in which there are many young children, and to all persons in weak health who may be contemplating Emigration, to postpone their departure until a milder season. There can be no doubt that the sea sickness consequent on the rough weather which Ships must encounter at this season, joined to the cold and damp of a sea voyage, will render persons who are not strong more susceptible to the attacks of this disease.

To those who may Emigrate at this season the Commissioners strongly recommend that they should provide themselves with as much warm clothing as they can, and especially with flannel, to be worn next the Skin; that they should have both their clothes and their persons quite clean before embarking, and should be careful to keep them so during the voyage,—and that they should provide themselves with as much solid and wholesome food as they can procure, in addition to the Ship's allowance to be used on the voyage. It would, of course, be desirable, if they can arrange it, that they should not go in a Ship that is much crowded, or that is not provided with a Medical Man.

By Order of the Board,

S. WALCOTT,
SECRETRAY.

Colonial Land and Emigration Office,
8, Park Street, Westminster,
November, 1853.

Under the feeble rays of a ship's lantern, a woman collapses on a steerage deck littered with sickly passengers. This woodcut appeared in an 1869 issue of Harper's Weekly that denounced living conditions aboard the packet ships. In a single run between Liverpool and New York that year, one vessel lost 20 lives to shipboard diseases.

when a potato famine starved Irish peasants in epic numbers, and landlords—in the phrase used at the time—"shoveled out" their tenants as quickly as they could.

The *Lord Ashburton* out of Liverpool that year lost 107 of its 475 steerage passengers to typhus during a crossing. The *Virginius*, carrying 596 in steerage, lost 158, and the ship's captain died the day after arrival. On the *Sir Henry Pottinger* 98 out of 399 were buried at sea, on the *Larch* 108 out of 440. "The Blackhole of Calcutta was a mercy compared to the holds of these vessels," *The Times* of London later reported. All told, of 250,000 emigrants who left the British Isles for North America that year, 20,000 died during the passage or shortly thereafter—the overwhelming majority of them from typhus. In the annals of the transatlantic migration, 1847 came to be known as the Year of the Plague.

A cabin passenger named Robert Whyte, traveling on a small vessel that left Dublin on May 30, 1847, left a vivid account of what it was like to sail with ship fever. The 110 emigrants who booked passage on the ship were visibly undernourished, he wrote, and "quite unfit to undergo the hardship of a long voyage." But they passed the perfunctory medical inspection and were taken aboard. On the 10th day out, two women fell seriously ill. By about the halfway mark, two cases of dysentery and six cases of ship fever had broken out. There was no doctor aboard the ship, so the captain's wife, who came to be known to the passengers as "the mistress," bravely stepped into the breach—despite the protests of her husband, who remonstrated in vain against her entering the disease-ridden steerage.

"The mistress was kept busy mixing medicine and making drinks, hoping that by early attention the sickness might be prevented from spreading," Whyte wrote. Her prescription for dysentery—flour porridge, with a few drops of laudanum—seemed to give the victims some relief. But there was little she could do for the ones who had typhus. To increase the distress of all aboard, some of the water casks were leaking, and the ship was also making less headway than expected. The captain had to ration both food and water.

In the meantime, the tally of fever cases had climbed to 30, with effects that were grievous to watch. One woman fell down senseless while she was warming a drink at the fire for her husband. A little girl at play suddenly dropped in a dead faint; when she regained consciousness, she started screaming and writhing convulsively. Whyte saw a woman with "feet swollen to double their natural size, and covered with black putrid spots." She soon died, and her body was thrown over the side into the Atlantic without ceremony. The dead woman's aunt "continued to gaze upon the ocean as if she could mark the spot where the waters opened for their prey."

Ringing in a new shipbuilding era

Many of the emigrants who crossed the Atlantic aboard packet ships later found work in the shipbuilding trade—often in the yards where the packets were built. There they made an enduring contribution to the lot of their fellow laborers.

During the packet era, the center of shipbuilding lay along Manhattan's East River, where more than a dozen yards ultimately turned out 160 vessels for the transatlantic routes. Yard owners made their own rules and often kept carpenters, joiners and calkers on the job from sunup until dark (in summer that meant from 4:30 a.m. until 7:30 p.m.). The workers, collectively known—like many 19th Century skilled workers—as mechanics, earned $1.25 a day. That was a living wage, when room and board cost five dollars a month, but hardly overgenerous considering the time put in.

Then came the emigrants, fleeing oppressive working conditions in Europe and emboldened by idealistic notions about American freedom. They fully expected that, in America, workers would set the standards of labor—and their attitude proved contagious. In 1831, mechanics at three adjacent yards banded together and unilaterally cut their workday to 10 hours.

For reasons that are unrecorded, the owners of the yards acceded to the change. They also accepted a device that prevented any boss from cheating on the hours: The workers erected a 25-foot tower topped by an 18-inch brass bell, which was rung six times a day—at 6 a.m. to start work, at the beginning and end of one-hour breakfast and lunch breaks, and at 6 p.m. as the call to go home.

Inevitably, pressure for better working conditions spread, spurred by the bell's daily reminders of the power of labor solidarity. In 1833, workers all over the waterfront campaigned for shorter hours. The yard owners offered a raise to two dollars a day if workers would keep to the old hours, but the mechanics held to their demand—and gave it sting in the form of sporadic strikes. The owners, fearing the loss of their skilled employees as much as the stoppages, agreed to the shorter day. A little later, they were persuaded to concede the two-dollar daily wage too.

In 1834 the workers lifted a new standard above the waterfront—a 36-inch Mechanics' Bell whose clarion call resounded to distant yards. Over the next 63 years, the bell was moved as the centers of shipbuilding shifted, but its tolling continued to herald the beginning and end of the workday until the industry died out on the East River at the end of the 19th Century.

At last, after 34 days, the vessel reached the Grand Banks, off New-foundland, in a dense fog on July 3. As she ghosted along the coast, the tolling bells of fishing vessels were heard. To warn them of her presence, the emigrant ship sounded mournful blasts with her foghorn. But to Whyte's ears a more desolate sound in the enveloping mist was the delirious wailing of 37 typhus victims.

By July 22, the ship had entered the St. Lawrence River. The supply of fresh water was now running so low that the steerage passengers were ordered to use the saline river water for cooking, and several patients who hitherto had seemed to be rallying suffered a relapse. Thanks to the ministrations of the captain's wife—and no little luck—only six of the passengers had died. But when the voyage ended after nearly two months, a dozen passengers remained dangerously sick and had to be separated from their families for hospitalization. At the parting, "the screams pierced my brain," Whyte wrote. "O God! may I never again witness such a scene."

Since the 1830s, when cholera-ridden ships had begun dumping boat-loads of diseased arrivals on the western shore of the Atlantic, the citizens of the New World had tried various means of self-protection. In Canada, Grosse Ile, located approximately 350 miles up the St. Lawrence River, had been designated a quarantine station for the examination of ships en route to Quebec and Montreal. Similar facilities existed to the

The Mechanics' Bell stands guard over the East River. The bell was melted down during World War II to provide metal for weaponry.

south, at Boston, Philadelphia and New York. The quarantine stations were intended as a final barrier against the indiscriminate spread of disease from ship to shore; more often than not, however, the barrier proved to be a sieve.

The inspection of passengers aboard the arriving ships was as cursory as the medical examination they had received before departing from Liverpool, for the simple reason that the volume of people to be inspected was overwhelming. During the height of the transatlantic migration, 1,600 ships arrived every year, many of them with 1,000 passengers aboard. And not everyone was inspected. Captains were generally unwilling to face a possible month's detention if disease was found on their ship—so they would resort to any ruse to avoid the sentence, hiding sick passengers away on the ship or dropping them off somewhere along the coast of New Jersey. And even when inspectors did detain a vessel for 30 days, the emigrants would sometimes jump ship and head into New York in small lighters.

Infection could be spread by objects as well as by people. As a ship came into the harbor, the passengers would throw their bedding and rubbish overboard; this flotsam would eventually wash up on the island with the tide, where it was collected by scavengers. Anything serviceable was later taken into the city and sold, transmitting whatever deadly microorganisms it contained.

In reaction to the ever-growing health problem, the port of New York tightened up its quarantine laws in early 1847; among other things, an emigration commission was empowered to collect a head tax of $1.50 per passenger coming into the port, the money to be put toward maintaining the quarantine station and its hospital. The tax—a stiff one—effectively barred some of the poorest emigrants. But it did little to help other packet ports. When incoming packet ships discovered that they would have difficulty unloading at New York, they changed course and headed for Montreal and Quebec. That year the quarantine station at Grosse Ile virtually collapsed under the onslaught.

Dr. George Douglas, the island's medical superintendent, had a staff that consisted of one steward, one orderly and one nurse when he opened the quarantine station on May 4, 1847. The hospital could accommodate 200 patients. Ten days later the first ship of the season, the *Syria* from Liverpool, arrived with 243 passengers aboard, 52 of whom were ill. Nine other persons had died during the voyage. The *Syria*'s 10th death occurred at Grosse Ile the day after she arrived in port. As the days passed, the plague ships kept coming. By the 28th of May, there were 856 cases of typhus and dysentery on the island, with another 470 still aboard ships anchored in the roadsteads. Thirty-six more vessels, containing a total of 13,000 passengers, awaited inspection. The sick and the dying overflowed the hospital and were cared for in hastily erected shanties and tents. Dr. Douglas tried frantically to enlist a staff of physicians, nurses and orderlies, but some refused to come, and of the 26 he did manage to hire by the middle of June, 23 fell ill in less than three weeks. At no time did he have enough healthy people to take care of the sick—or to dig the graves of those who died.

On June 8 the doctor wrote a somber letter to the chief emigration

A cartoon pokes fun at cabin passengers. Acquiring sea legs was an unnerving experience. "Amongst the pea Soup were the passengers rolling on deck messing and sprawling like pigs," wrote one traveler. "Spoiled all their clothes."

Mr. Slim is behind time, and has to take a boat in order to reach the vessel.

He reaches the ship, but finds some difficulty in getting on board.

A hundred miles out at sea. Squally. He thinks he will go to his state-room.

Mr. Slim in his state-room.—Position Number Two

agent at Quebec. "Out of the 4,000 or 5,000 emigrants that have left this island since Sunday," he warned, "at least 2,000 will fall sick somewhere before three weeks are over. They ought to have accommodation for 2,000 sick at least at Montreal and Quebec, as all the Cork and Liverpool passengers are half dead from starvation and want before embarking." For people who had made the ocean crossing in search of a better future, they presented a melancholy sight. "I never saw people so indifferent to life," Douglas wrote, adding that on the ships, he had been told, "they would continue in the same berth with a dead person until the seamen or captain dragged out the corpse with boathooks."

By the end of the year, Douglas reported, a total of 8,691 stricken emigrants had been treated in the island's facilities; 5,424 of them had died. Besides the emigrants, there were another 44 casualties: members of the hospital staff.

The tragedy on the emigrant ships might have been prevented, or at least mitigated, if the various Passenger Vessel Acts in force at the time had been observed—if brokers had not sold tickets to more passengers than a ship was supposed to carry, if the preembarkation medical examinations had been thorough, if captains had refused to allow sick passengers to come aboard their vessels. In 1855 an outraged and frightened citizenry at the receiving end of the transatlantic migration pressured Congress into passing yet more laws, this time with a new twist that threatened the captains and, through them, the shipowners. Captains would be fined a stiff $50 for every passenger they carried in excess of their allotment, and another $10 for the death of every passenger who was more than eight years of age. But this law had no more effect than its predecessors. The authorities turned a blind eye to well-documented violations that could have cost individual captains tens of thousands of dollars.

In the face of such neglect by shipowners, captains, crews and law-enforcement agents, transatlantic emigration continued without letup. There was no denying that the emigrants were better off in the new country, and they wrote glowing letters to their relatives back home. "We all have plenty of work to do here," said one, adding: "You know the state we were in when we left you—we had neither meat nor money—but we have plenty of everything that we need at present." Another wrote: "Urge my brothers to come out if ever they wish to free themselves from bondage; this is the land of independence to the industrious." And a third: "By adopting this country as the future home of myself and family, I am now a *master*, where I could never well expect otherwise than to see myself and my family as *servants*."

Nor was the act of getting to America invariably a traumatic experience. On some ships, steerage passengers dealt with adversity by organizing themselves into mutual-aid societies that cared for the sick and guarded against theft. Emigrants also took steps to protect women from the unwanted attentions of the crew or other voyagers. If a female passenger was not traveling in the company of a father or brother, her family would attempt to enlist some other chaperon beforehand—perhaps a trusted neighbor who was making the trip.

Feels somewhat uneasy, but, thinking dinner will do him good, takes his seat at the table.

Feeling a little better, he proceeds on deck. Curious aspect of things in general.

Odd feeling comes over him. Thinks he will go back to his state-room.

Mr. Slim in his state-room again. Wonders if he is going to be sea-sick.

Chaperonage did not, of course, rule out innocent fun, and many an evening was brightened with the sounds of music. Fiddlers would strike up a tune, dancers would leap into jigs and reels. A passenger who sailed aboard the *John Dennison* recalled that the quarter-deck would be cleared every evening at 6 o'clock, and the ship's surgeon would set to on the fiddle. With the ship's baker performing the role of master of ceremonies, and with a gallon of rum purchased from the ship's steward, "the dance and merriment were kept up with great spirit until four bells, or 10 p.m. Many more bottles besides the gallon were drunk."

Cabin passengers lounge around the capstan as a puppy watches from an abandoned shuffleboard court. By the 1830s, packet owners routinely provided shipboard games for the well-to-do passengers who were taking up travel for enlightenment and relaxation.

Even at their merriest, steerage festivities were but a pale reflection of the amusements afforded the passengers elsewhere on the ship—those who paid 10 times as much as the emigrants to travel cabin-class. Included in their ranks were businessmen, lecturers and actors who earned handsome sums touring America, and all manner of other voyagers who were curious about the New World and had the time and money to indulge their interest. Curiosity operated in both directions, of course. From Boston and New York a new generation of Americans sailed eastward to explore Europe; intercontinental tourism had begun.

Although cabin and steerage passengers were only a deck apart, their lives aboard ship could not have been more different. The cabin passengers usually knew about the grim conditions below only by hearsay, and even if they had wanted to get at the facts, personal investigation was not always possible. On the *Hottinguer* in 1845, Mrs. Sarah Mytton Maury recorded that the ship's doctor refused to let her go down into the steerage, "holding it not only dangerous and unwholesome, but as being a spectacle wholly unfit for the eyes of a female unaccustomed to behold the strange, and sorry, and demoralizing economy which prevails in those dens of disease and misery." So, while the steerage passenger fought for a place at a cooking grate to prepare his oatmeal or tossed fitfully in his lice-ridden bunk, cabin passengers like Mrs. Maury were often oblivious of the plight of their fellow travelers. They themselves were waited on by skilled stewards, or played quoits on deck to work up an appetite for the next lengthy meal.

In cabin class, luxury was ubiquitous. "The ladies' cabin is distinguished by the extreme elegance of the fittings," effused a journalist who examined the packet *Victoria* in 1843. "Indeed, no drawing-room or boudoir on *terra firma* presents a nicer specimen of decorative art or appropriate upholstery. The style of the apartment is that of Louis Quatorze or Quinze, in the most delicate white and gold, the carved framework of the panels being well executed."

Eleven years later another reporter described the equally elegant dining saloon on the *Marco Polo*: "It is ceiled with maple and the pilasters are panelled with richly ornamented and silvered glass," he noted, "coins of various countries being a novel feature of the decorations." The upholstery was done in embossed crimson velvet.

The food provided for the cabin passengers was no less lavish. As described by a traveler aboard the packet *Ontario* in the early 1830s, it seemed to pour forth from the ship's galley in an almost ceaseless stream. Breakfast, served at 9 o'clock, consisted of "black tea, green tea, coffee, biscuit, bread, hot rolls, fish, fowl, ham, cold mutton, eggs," wrote William Lyon Mackenzie. And sometimes there would be chocolate as well. Lunch featured an impressive spread of cold meats. At four in the afternoon came a dinner that could go on for hours: "soups, fresh mutton, beef, pork and sometimes veal, barn-door fowls, bacon, plum-pudding, preserves, pastry." A variety of nuts and fruit were offered for dessert. As for libations, "excellent madeira and port, and also claret, are always on the table, and occasionally (say, every other day) champagne, a very fair and genuine sample, is served round after the cloth is removed."

In between the main meals were other occasions for refreshment. There might be a midmorning glass of port, taken on deck in fair weather. At seven or eight in the evening on some ships, the stewards presented a meal called tea—a repeat of the lunch. And just before retiring, a traveler might partake of sardines and toast.

When they were not at table, the cabin passengers sought and found a variety of amusements to pass the time. Some might spend hours shooting with rifles and pistols at bottles suspended from a spar, or trying to tempt sharks into following the ship by throwing pieces of beef and mutton over the side. On rare occasions, passengers would get an opportunity to shoot at polar bears on drifting icebergs. Sometimes a member of the crew would harpoon a porpoise, and the ship's cooks would then

Two passengers—one unaccountably dressed in his dinner jacket—lie abed in a packet cabin. Such luxuries as separate bunks and a carpet on the floor made their appearance as early as 1819 but were available to only the richest travelers; of all those who emigrated from Great Britain to the United States between the Revolutionary War and 1890, scarcely 2 per cent could afford cabin passage.

concoct a feast based on this exotic flesh. Rat hunts—a serious concern in steerage—were pure sport for cabin passengers. When the sea was calm, some adventuresome souls would dive overboard and swim around the ship. "For the want of work," one of them reflected, the men on board "turned boys again, and went to play."

For travelers with more sedate tastes, a similarly broad range of amusements was available. Some of the more luxurious vessels provided professional orchestras for evening concerts and dances. And on every ship, cabin passengers whiled away the hours at checkers, chess, dominoes, backgammon, whist and poker (a game that reputedly originated in the American hinterland and found its way to England via packet). Passengers also laid bets on the distance covered by the ship each day—a tradition that would be carried on by the ocean liners—and on the time of their ship's arrival in port.

On the *Pacific* in 1832 "a society was established for the good demeanor and sociability of the passengers," wrote the actress Fanny Kemble, and under the direction of its elected officers this group played popular guessing games such as "dumb crambo, and earth, air and water, with

The Irish comic actor Tyrone Power (inset) sailed to New York in 1833 aboard the packet Europe. To Power, the vessel was a floating stage and its passengers a captive audience—and not surprisingly, he enjoyed himself. He exhorted friends to take a packet voyage. "Forgive your enemies, kiss your wife," he said, "and with a clean heart, backed by forty-eight clean shirts, go and try it."

The White Diamond Line's packet
Washington Irving carried the American
author Ralph Waldo Emerson (inset)
to England in 1847 for what he expected
would be "a change and a tonic."
The voyage gave the philosopher plenty
of time to think; he spent it musing
darkly about "the dread of the sea" and
opined: "The wonder is always
new that any sane man can be a sailor."

infinite zeal." The English novelist Charles Dickens, who made a crossing on the George Washington in 1842, was also a member of an impromptu club—"to whose distinguished president modesty forbids me to make any further allusion." It was, he said, "a very hilarious and jovial institution." The clubs took great pleasure in staging mock trials and debates, as well as amateur theatricals.

Meeting another ship at sea was always an occasion. If it was passing in the opposite direction, passengers might hurl weighted messages for home across the water. Overtaking, or being passed by, a rival packet was an even greater cause of excitement. One day during her crossing aboard the United States in 1834, the English social reformer Harriet Martineau directed the captain's attention to another sail. "He snatched his glass," she recorded, "and the next moment electrified us all by the vehemence of his directions to the helmsman and others of the crew." The ship turned out to be a rival packet, the Montreal, which had left Portsmouth four days ahead of the United States. "We were in for a race," Miss Martineau wrote. The Montreal was faster in a light wind, the United States in a strong wind. As usual on the Atlantic, strong

A packet disembarks passengers onto the New York waterfront, bustling with arrivals from the world over—including some who came on the Keying (background), the first Chinese junk to visit America. By 1855, one of four emigrants was Irish, an influx lampooned at right by a trunk labeled "Pat Murfy For Ameriky."

winds prevailed, and the *United States* beat the *Montreal* to New York by a margin Miss Martineau neglected to chronicle.

In every way—whether by seamanly panache or his deportment while presiding over meals—the captain set the tone of the ship. Packet captains mingled as equals with even the most prominent voyagers. They showed important guests around the ship, and had to be skilled diplomats who could flatter the vanities of one important traveler without slighting another.

These efforts were often rewarded with imaginative expressions of thanks. Sometimes the tributes took the form of expensive gifts. Napoleon's brother Joseph, King of Spain from 1808 to 1813, sailed three times with a jaunty Connecticut Yankee named Elisha E. Morgan, who was captain of the *Philadelphia*. As a token of thanks for the attentions he had received, Joseph presented Morgan with a chessboard that had been used by Napoleon at St. Helena, and a silver tea-and-coffee service and set of gold cutlery that Napoleon had given to his mother.

Other tokens of esteem might be less lavish though no less heady for the captain. The passengers of the Black Ball liner *Columbia* placed a notice in the New York newspapers attesting to Captain William Lee's "assiduous attention and gentlemanlike conduct" on a voyage they had taken under his command. Doubtless the most novel tribute was paid to Captain David G. Bailey, who brought the *Yorkshire* from Liverpool to New York in a record-setting 16 days in 1846. Among his passengers were the youthful members of a Viennese ballet troupe. "Those beautiful children were so delighted with him and his ship," reported the *New York Herald*, "that they danced the splendid *Pas de Fleurs* on his quarter deck coming up the harbor."

Not every cabin passenger rejoiced in sea travel, of course. New England philosopher Ralph Waldo Emerson was a less-than-enthusiastic sailor. "I waked every morning with the belief that someone was tipping my berth," Emerson wrote, describing an ocean crossing he made in 1847. "Nobody likes to be treated ignominiously, upset, shoved against the side of the house, rolled over, suffocated with bilge, mephitis and stewing oil." The best he could say for sea life was that it was "an acquired taste, like that for tomatoes and olives."

Harriet Martineau found the ordeal of a storm intolerable. "All night the noises would have banished sleep if we could have lain quiet," she wrote. "There was a roar of wind; the waves dashed against the side of the ship as if they were bursting in; water poured into our cabin, though the skylight was fastened down." With her belongings lying in wet heaps all around, Miss Martineau staggered through the ladies' cabin in search of a dry place to sleep. The only place that she could find was underneath the table. "So I brought a blanket and pillow, laid down with a firm hold of the leg of the table, and got an hour's welcome sleep, by which time the storm was enough to have wakened the dead."

The same Miss Martineau—who was once characterized by a contemporary as "that dyspeptic Radical battle-axe" for her vigorous crusades to pass laws protecting English paupers—looked on the cabin passengers' sumptuous fare with bluenosed disapproval. "Some of us felt it rather annoying to be so long at table," she wrote. "But it is a custom

Protective welcome for the newcomers

Immigrants relax in Castle Garden's rotunda, stop by an information desk, purchase tickets and meet friends.

As the migration to America rose to flood proportions in the middle years of the 19th Century, many of the men and women pouring onto the Manhattan docks received a disastrous introduction to the New World. If they were not met by relatives or friends, they found themselves beset by dubious Samaritans known as runners, who sold them fraudulent railroad tickets to their destinations and charged up to $10 to haul their baggage—then disappeared with it.

In 1855, New York finally acted to halt such predatory practices: That year, the world's first immigrant landing depot was opened at Castle Garden in Manhattan's Battery section. Built in 1807 as a fort and later used as a concert hall, Castle Garden now came to be known as the "Nation's Gateway," and through it 7,690,606 foreigners would pass during the next four decades.

Its services were numerous. In the depot, travel specialists handed out maps and helped the newcomers plan journeys to their prospective homes. Railroad tickets were sold by authorized agents. Food for the trip could be bought at wholesale prices and cooked in the depot's kitchens. A so-called labor exchange—in effect, an employment agency—helped find jobs for the settlers. And, somewhat reluctantly, Castle Garden even offered a modicum of shelter. Although immigration authorities hoped travelers would use the depot as a one-day stopover and provided no beds, as many as 3,000 people sometimes stretched out on the floor for a night.

For all its good intentions, the depot ran into trouble. The railway agents, unable to resist easy money, began charging more than face value for tickets and pocketing the difference. Money-changers, taking advantage of foreigners' ignorance about American currency, sometimes gave a handful of shiny pennies in exchange for European money worth much more. By 1890, the problems had become so severe that Castle Garden was replaced by a more rigorously controlled "Nation's Gateway" on Ellis Island, in New York Bay. The old depot closed its doors, underwent yet another refurbishing, and reopened as a public aquarium.

established on board these packets, for the sake, I believe, of those who happen to find the day too long."

A phenomenon that could certainly make the hours seem to drag was a dead calm: The absence of any discernible forward movement of the ship took a toll on nerves. "If there be an infirmity of temper," Miss Martineau wrote, "it is sure to come out then. At such a time, there is much playing of shuffleboard upon deck, and the matches do not always end harmoniously." Even a game of cards or chess could get tense. "There may be heard a subdued tone of scolding from the whist party at the top of the table, and a stray oath from some checkmated person lower down." Moreover, she added darkly, there were episodes of backbiting among the ladies "brushing their hair in their cabin."

One cabin passenger whose spirits never drooped was Tyrone Power, an actor whose repeated crossings made him a familiar figure on both sides of the Atlantic. No philosopher, but a robust man with a keen appetite for food and drink and the funny side of life, Power delighted in virtually everything aboard a packet ship. Bounding from his stateroom at 6 o'clock in the morning, he would run out on deck in his cotton drawers—"sunshine or cloud, calm or squall"—to keep an appointment with "a grim-looking seven-foot seaman" waiting with a couple of buckets of sea water. "With a half-grin," Power recalled, this ominous

A coal-burning challenger takes to sea

Only a few years after packets established themselves on the run between New York and Liverpool, a few farsighted shipowners began to wonder if steamships might not bring a further measure of maritime regularity to Atlantic commerce. Steamships, after all, were almost immune to the caprices of the wind, and they had long since proved their reliability in coastal and river trade. But could their engines stand the strain of such a long-distance passage? Said one skeptic, "They might as well talk of making a voyage from New York or Liverpool to the moon."

Junius Smith, a Connecticut-born merchant who operated out of London, ignored such naysaying. In 1832, he sailed to New York on a packet—spending a wearisome 54 days en route—to seek backers for a transatlantic steamship line. Finding none among his usually venturesome countrymen, he returned to London, where he successfully recruited investors. In 1835 he announced the founding of the British and American Steam Navigation Company. By early 1838, his first ship, the 1,850-ton British Queen, was nearing completion. The contest between steam and sail was on.

But Smith himself had challengers. The Great Western Steamship Company, organized in Bristol a year after Smith's line, was planning to send its new steamship Great Western across the Atlantic. When construction of the Brit-

ish Queen began to lag, Smith chartered a smaller steamer, the Sirius, and sent her off instead. On April 23, 1838, the Sirius chugged into New York, the first ship to cross by steam alone. She almost had to share the honor: The Great Western docked in New York only eight hours later.

Within months, Smith's British Queen was operating on the London-New York run, averaging 16 days westbound and 14 days eastbound—twice as fast as many sailing packets. In 1840, Smith launched the 2,866-ton President, the largest and most elegant ship on the seas. Accolades poured in, and it was rumored that the "Yankee Innovator"—as the British press called him—was in line for knighthood.

Then came tragedy. In 1841 the President went down, taking with her all 136 aboard—including actor Tyrone Power. The company's reputation was ruined. Smith sold the British Queen and retired to a tea plantation in South Carolina. In 1851, at the age of 70, he was badly beaten by ruffians who opposed his antislavery views. He never recovered, dying in 1853.

At the time of his death, sailing packets still reigned on the Atlantic, but steamship operators like Samuel Cunard would bring Smith's vision to fruition. In shipping, Smith used to say, "dispatch is the life and delay the death"—a motto whose truth guaranteed the ultimate victory of steam.

giant with a puckered face would bless "the simplicity of the landsman" who turned out every morning "to be soused like the captain's turtle."

But for Power, the pleasure of an invigorating bath was "light in comparison with the after enjoyment." When the steward's bell signaled breakfast, Power would be ready. "It is worth a life of ordinary vegetation to be stirred but for once" by a packet breakfast, he rhapsodized.

After a day full of splendid meals and such diversions as a bit of whist with the ladies in their cabin—"a pretty square apartment," he wrote, "fitted up with sofas, mirrors and other little elegancies"— Power was back on deck with a nightcap. "Give the last half of your grog to the old lad at the wheel," he suggested. "Peep in on the compass, find she heads about west-north-west, and, well satisfied, descend the stair." There, in the cabin, the final curtain would fall on a day wellspent: "The steward lights the waxen taper which fixes on a branch before your glass; when, having performed such ceremonies as you delight in, thank God and sleep."

But the excitement of making landfall exceeded everything else, and Power was even willing to surrender his sleep to share in it. Traveling to America on board the *Europe* in 1833, he went to bed before the vessel reached port, but left a call with the captain to rouse him if land was sighted. At three in the morning he tumbled out on deck to spy the lights

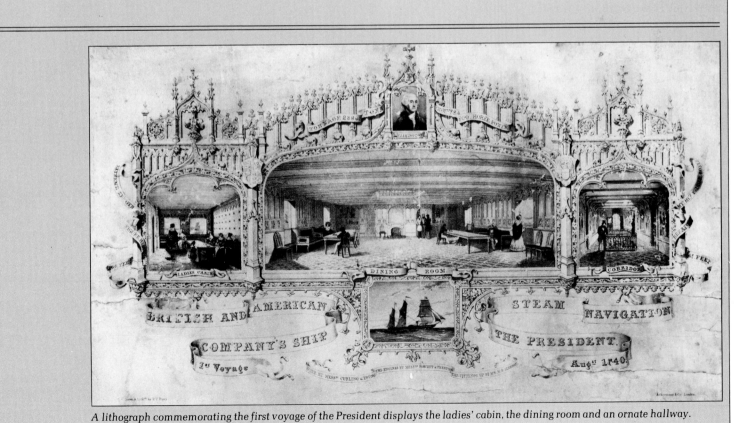

A lithograph commemorating the first voyage of the President displays the ladies' cabin, the dining room and an ornate hallway.

on Sandy Hook that marked the outer edge of New York harbor. The ship sent up skyrockets, signaling for a pilot, who won the hearts of the cabin travelers by presenting them with a basket of fresh-caught fish, just in time for a final—and appropriately grand—breakfast.

That cabin passengers like Power could find such pleasures at sea underscored the changes that had come over Atlantic travel since the frail little *Mayflower* had pioneered the ocean crossing more than 200 years before. Scarcely 100 souls had braved that passage; by the middle of the 19th Century an average of more than a quarter of a million passengers were making the trip annually, and in peak years the total approached half a million. The *Mayflower* had been a diminutive 180 tons; packet tonnage for 1860 totaled more than 975,000. The *Mayflower*'s cargo of kettles, guns and axes represented the bare essentials of livelihood in a wilderness; now packet ships carried sophisticated cargoes that ranged from railroad tracks forged in British steel mills to wines made in France.

Yet a shadow lay across their future. Steamship lines had first begun to operate on the Atlantic run in 1838, and by the middle of the 19th Century, even as emigrants at Liverpool swarmed aboard outbound square-riggers in record numbers, British and American steamships were taking on the function of bearing news, mail and fine freight. More and more comfort-loving cabin passengers began switching to steam as well. Dickens and P. T. Barnum were among the many who took a sailing packet for the speedy eastward passage to Europe—but made the trip to America aboard one of the Cunard Line's steamships, because they moved faster against the prevailing westerlies.

At first, the steamers scornfully left the emigrant trade to the "canvasbacks." But that situation changed dramatically after the steamship *City of Glasgow* turned a nice profit in 1850 by carrying 400 souls in steerage. By 1863, forty-five per cent of British emigrants to the New World came by steam; three years later, the figures had increased to 81 per cent.

Still, the sailing packets, making do with heavy cargoes such as grain and coal, hung on for a time; the major lines were still operating after the Civil War. But three of the five largest—the Red Star, Blue Swallowtail and Dramatic Lines—all closed down before 1878. At the start of 1878, the year of the Black Ball Line's 60th anniversary, the pioneering company was still running a full service of six ships to Liverpool. Then at the end of the summer it too shut down.

The Red Swallowtail Line was the last of the packet lines to go. Throughout the summer of 1880 it maintained its regular schedules. But in September the *Sir Robert Peel* was sold and sent to Trieste for a career as a merchantman. In November the *Liverpool*—after completing a record 37 years of Atlantic packet service—was sold as well, and headed for Bordeaux.

One by one, like the family heirlooms of an impoverished household, the oceangoing packets were cashed in. The last one to cross the Atlantic arrived in New York from London on May 18, 1881. She was a 1,396-ton vessel, built of good white oak in Thomaston, Maine, 18 years before. No record survives of the goods she carried, but it is hard to forget her name. She was called the *Ne Plus Ultra*—"Nothing Further."

In a scene captured in 1907 by the great photographer Alfred Stieglitz, emigrants assemble on the deck of a steamship as others gather their clothes below in preparation for arrival in New York harbor. By the opening decade of the 20th Century, steamers had replaced sailing packets, but European emigrants were still crossing the Atlantic at the rate of a million a year.

Bibliography

Abbot, Edith, *Immigration: Select Documents and Case Records.* University of Chicago Press, 1924.

Albion, Robert G.:
"Planning the Black Ball." *The Log of Mystic Seaport,* Spring 1980.
The Rise of New York Port. Charles Scribner's Sons, 1939.
Square-Riggers on Schedule. Archon Books, 1965.

Allan, Herbert S., *John Hancock: Patriot in Purple.* Beechhurst Press, 1953.

Allen, Edward L., *Pilot Lore from Steam to Sail.* United New York and New Jersey Sandy Hook Pilot's Benevolent Association, 1922.

Allen, Gardner W., *A Naval History of the American Revolution,* Vols. 1, 2. Russell & Russell, 1962.

Allen, George F., *Francis' Metallic Life-Boat Company.* William C. Bryant, 1852.

American and Commercial Daily Advertiser. Baltimore: June 1, 1822.

Ames, Azel, *The Mayflower and Her Log.* Riverside Press, 1901.

Arber, Edward, and A. G. Bradley, eds., *Travels and Works of Captain John Smith.* 2 vols. Edinburgh: John Grant, 1910.

Asbury, Herbert, *Ye Olde Fire Laddies.* Alfred A. Knopf, 1930.

Baker, William A., *Colonial Vessels: Some Seventeenth-Century Sailing Craft.* Barre Publishing, 1962.

Barbour, Philip L., *The Three Worlds of Captain John Smith.* Riverside Press, 1964.

Bartlett, Robert Merrill, *The Pilgrim Way.* Pilgrim Press, 1971.

Baxter, W. T., *The House of Hancock.* Harvard University Press, 1945.

Bennett, Robert F., *The Lifesaving Service at Sandy Hook Station 1854-1915.* U.S. Coast Guard Historical Monograph Program, 1976.

Bining, Arthur C., and Thomas C. Cochran, *The Rise of American Economic Life.* 4th ed. Charles Scribner's Sons, 1964.

Bonfanti, Leo, *The Witchcraft Hysteria of 1692,* Vols. 1, 2. Pride Publications, 1971.

Bradford, William, *Of Plymouth Plantation 1620-1647.* Ed. by Samuel Eliot Morison. Alfred A. Knopf, 1979.

Briggs, Rose T., *Plymouth Rock: History and Significance.* Nimrod Press, 1968.

Brinnin, John Malcolm, *The Sway of the Grand Saloon: A Social History of the North Atlantic.* Delacorte Press, 1971.

Brooks, Jerome E., *The Mighty Leaf: Tobacco through the Centuries.* Little, Brown, 1952.

Bunker, John G., *Harbor and Haven, an Illustrated History of the Port of New York.* Windsor Publications, 1979.

The Burning of the Ship Ocean Monarch, with a Full Account of Frederick Jerome. G. E. and C. W. Kenworthy, 1849.

Butler, William Allen, *Memorial of Charles Marshall.* D. Appleton, 1867.

Caffrey, Kate, *The Mayflower.* Stein and Day, 1974.

Campbell, John F., *History and Bibliography of the New American Practical Navigator and the American Coast Pilot.* Peabody Museum of Salem, 1964.

Capron, Walter C., *The U.S. Coast Guard.* Franklin Watts, 1965.

Chandler, Charles Lyon, Marion V. Brewington and Edgar P. Richardson, *Philadelphia, Port of History.* Philadelphia Maritime Museum.

Chapelle, Howard I., *The Search for Speed under Sail.* Bonanza Books, 1967.

The City of New York. Museum of the City of New York, 1978.

Coleman, Terry:
Going to America. Doubleday, 1973.
Passage to America. London: Hutchinson, 1972.

Compston, H.F.B., *Thomas Coram: Churchman, Empire Builder, Philanthropist.* Society for Promoting Christian Knowledge, 1918.

Cope, Thomas P., *Philadelphia Merchant: The Diary of Thomas P. Cope, 1800-1851.* Gateway Editions, 1978.

Costello, Augustine E., *Our Firemen: A History of the New York Fire Departments.* Costello, 1887.

Cowan, Helen L., *British Emigration to British North America: The First Hundred Years.* University of Toronto Press, 1961.

Cutler, Carl C., *Queens of the Western Ocean.* United States Naval Institute, 1961.

Dickens, Charles, *American Notes.* Peter Smith, 1968.

Dictionary of American Biography. Ed. by Allen Johnson and Dumas Malone. Scribner's Sons.

Durant, John and Alice, *Pictorial History of American Ships on the High Seas and Inland Waters.* A. S. Barnes, 1953.

The Editors of Time-Life Books, *The History of the United States,* Vol. 3. Time-Life Books, 1963.

Ehrhardt, John B., *Joseph Francis—1801-1893—Shipbuilder; Father of the U.S. Life-Saving Service.* The Newcomen Society in North America, 1950.

Emerson, Ralph Waldo, *English Traits.* Houghton Mifflin, 1885.

"Emigrants at Constitution Wharf, Boston." *Ballou's Pictorial,* October 31, 1857.

The Encyclopedia of Discovery and Exploration: The Conquest of North America. Doubleday, 1971.

Engle, Eloise and Arnold S. Lott, *America's Maritime Heritage.* Naval Institute Press, 1975.

Fairburn, William Armstrong, *Merchant Sail.* 6 vols. Fairburn Marine Educational Foundation, 1945-1955.

Faulkner, Harold Underwood, *American Economic History.* Harper & Brothers, 1949.

Forbes, R. B., *Notes on Some Few of the Wrecks and Rescues during the Present Century.* Little, Brown, 1889.

Francis' Metallic Life-Boat Company. William C. Bryant, 1852.

Gibbs, C. R. Vernon, *Passenger Liners of the Western Ocean.* London: Staples Press, 1957.

Goldenberg, Joseph A., *Shipbuilding in Colonial America.* University Press of Virginia for the Mariners Museum, 1976.

Greenhill, Basil, *The Great Migration: Crossing the Atlantic under Sail.* London: Her Majesty's Stationery Office, 1968.

Greenhill, Basil, and Ann Giffard, *Travelling by Sea in the Nineteenth Century.* Hastings House Publishers, 1974.

Griffith, Lucille, *Alabama, Documentary History to 1900.* University of Alabama Press, 1972.

Guillet, Edwin, *The Great Migration: The Atlantic Crossing by Sailing-Ship since 1770.* University of Toronto Press, 1963.

Hall, Michael G., *Edward Randolph and the American Colonies.* W. W. Norton, 1960.

Hansen, Marcus Lee, *The Atlantic Migration, 1607-1860.* Harper & Brothers, 1961.

Hawke, David, *The Colonial Experience.* Bobbs-Merrill, 1966.

Heimann, Robert K., *Tobacco and Americans.* McGraw-Hill, 1960.

Henderson, Welles J., and Leonard A. Swann Jr., *The Greater Port of Philadelphia Past, Present and Future.* Philadelphia Maritime Museum.

Herndon, G. Melvin, *William Tatham and the Culture of Tobacco.* University of Miami Press, 1969.

Hone, Philip, *The Diary of Philip Hone, 1822-1851,* Vol. 1. Ed. by Bayard Tuckerman. Dodd, Mead, 1889.

Hugill, Stan, *Sailortown.* E. P. Dutton, 1967.

Hulton, Paul, and David Beers Quinn, *The American Drawings of John White.* 2 vols. London and Chapel Hill: The Trustees of the British Museum and University of North Carolina Press, 1964.

Jones, Charles C., Jr., *The Dead Towns of Georgia.* Morning News Steam Printing House, 1878.

Jones, Maldwyn Allen, *American Immigration.* University of Chicago Press, 1960.

Kenworthy, G. E. and C. W., *The Burning of the Ship Ocean Monarch.* Kenworthy, 1849.

Laing, Alexander:
American Sail. E. P. Dutton, 1961.
Seafaring America. American Heritage Publishing, 1974.

Lever, Darcy, *The Young Sea Officer's Sheet Anchor.* E. & G. W. Blunt, 1843.

Lounsbury, Ralph G., *The British Fishery at Newfoundland 1634-1763.* Archon Books, 1969.

Lubbock, Basil, *The Western Ocean Packets.* Glasgow: Brown, Son & Ferguson,

171

1971.

Lyon, Jane D., *Clipper Ships and Captains.* American Heritage Publishing, 1962.

MacDonagh, Oliver, *A Pattern of Government Growth 1800-60.* London: MacGibbon & Kee, 1961.

McKay, Richard C., *South Street: A Maritime History of New York.* Haskell House Publishers, 1971.

Maclay, Edgar S., *A History of the American Privateers.* Books for Libraries Press, 1970.

Maritime History of New York. Haskell House Publishers, 1973.

Martineau, Harriet, *Retrospect of Western Travel,* Vol. 1. Haskell House Publishers, 1969.

Melville, Herman, *Redburn: His First Voyage.* Ed. by Harrison Hayford, Hersel Parker, and Thomas Tanselle. Northwestern University Press and the Newberry Library, 1969.

Middleton, Arthur Pierce, *Tobacco Coast: A Maritime History of Chesapeake Bay in the Colonial Era.* The Mariners Museum, 1953.

Moore, Francis, *A Voyage to Georgia Begun in the Year 1735.* London, 1744.

Morison, Samuel Eliot:
The Maritime History of Massachusetts. Riverside Press, 1961.
The Oxford History of the American People. Oxford University Press, 1965.

Morris, Ira K., *Morris's Memorial History of Staten Island.* Morris, 1900.

Morris, James M., *Our Maritime Heritage.* University Press of America, 1979.

Morris, John V., *Fires and Firefighters.* Bramhall House, 1955.

Morrison, John H., *History of New York Shipyards.* Kennikat Press, 1909.

Mossiker, Frances, *Pocahontas: The Life and the Legend.* Alfred A. Knopf, 1976.

Muir, Ramsay, *The History of Liverpool.* University Press of Liverpool, 1907.

Paine, Ralph D., *The Ships and Sailors of Old Salem.* Charles E. Lauriat, 1924.

Pomfret, John E., with Floyd M. Shumway, *Founding the American Colonies 1583-1660.* Harper & Row, 1970.

Pond, E. LeRoy, *Junius Smith: Pioneer Promoter of Transatlantic Steam Navigation.* The Marine Historical Association, 1941.

Pond, James L., ed., *History of Life-Saving Appliances and Military and Naval Constructions.* E. D. Slater, 1885.

Potter, George, *To the Golden Door, the Story of the Irish in Ireland and America.* Little, Brown.

Power, Tyrone, *Impressions of America during the Years 1833, 1834, and 1835,* Vol. 1. Benjamin Blom, 1971.

Quinn, David Beers, ed., *The Roanoke Voyages, 1584-1590.* 2 vols. London: The Hakluyt Society, 1955.

Rattray, Jeannette Edwards, *Perils of the Port of New York.* Dodd, Mead, 1973.

Reese, Trevor Richard, *Colonial Georgia.* University of Georgia Press, 1963.

Ritchie-Noakes, Nancy, *Jesse Hartley.* Liverpool: Merseyside County Museums, 1980.

Ross, Margorie Drake, *The Book of Boston.* Hastings House Publishers, 1964.

Rouse, Parke Jr.:
Planters and Pioneers: Life in Colonial Virginia. Hastings House Publishers, 1968.
Virginia: The English Heritage in America. Hastings House Publishers, 1966.

Russel, Charles Edward, *From Sandy Hook to 62°.* Century, 1929.

Samuels, Samuel, *From the Forecastle to the Cabin.* Harper & Brothers, 1887.

Schlesinger, Arthur M., *The Colonial Merchants and the American Revolution.* Frederick Ungar, 1957.

Shaw, Ronald E., *Erie Water West: A History of the Erie Canal, 1792-1854.* University of Kentucky Press, 1966.

Sheldon, George W.:
"The Old Packet and Clipper Service." *Harper's Magazine,* January 1884.
The Story of the Volunteer Fire Department of the City of New York. Harper & Brothers, 1882.

Shepherd, Barnett, *Sailors' Snug Harbor 1801-1976.* Publishing Center for Cultural Resources, 1979.

Sinclair, Harold, *The Port of New Orleans.* Doubleday, Doran, 1942.

Smith, Abbot Emerson, *Colonists in Bondage: White Servitude and Convict Labor in America, 1607-1776.* W. W. Norton, 1947.

Smith, Henry Justin, *The Master of the Mayflower.* Willett, Clark, 1936.

Smith, John, *New England Trials.* Ed. by Edward Arber. London: King's College, 1884.

Some Merchants and Sea Captains of Old Boston. State Street Trust Company, 1918.

Spears, John R., *Captain Nathaniel Brown Palmer, an Old-Time Sailor of the Sea.* Macmillan, 1922.

Staff, Frank, *The Transatlantic Mail.* Adlard Coles, 1956.

Stammers, Michael, *The Passage Makers.* Brighton: Teredo Books, 1978.

Taylor, Philip, *The Distant Magnet: European Emigration to the U.S.A.* London: Eyre & Spottiswoode, 1971.

Thomas, R., *Interesting and Authentic Narratives of the Most Remarkable Shipwrecks.* Books for Libraries Press, 1970.

The Times. London: January 10, 1839; January 14, 1839.

Timpus, Lowell M., *History of the New York Fire Department.* E. P. Dutton, 1940.

Umbreit, Kenneth, *Founding Fathers.* Kennikat Press, 1969.

Von Reck, Philip Georg Friedrich, *Von Reck's Voyages.* Ed. by Kristian Hvidt. The Beehive Press, 1980.

Wallace, Paul A. W., *Pennsylvania, Seed of a Nation.* Harper and Row, 1962.

Whyte, Robert, *The Ocean Plague: Or a Voyage to Quebec in an Irish Emigrant Vessel.* Coolidge and Wiley, 1848.

Willison, George F., *Saints and Strangers.* Time Reading Program Special Edition, Time Inc., 1964.

Wright, Louis B., *The Atlantic Frontier.* Cornell University Press, 1964.

Writers Program of New York, *A Maritime History of New York.* Haskell House Publishers, 1973.

Young, Harold E., *ByGone Liverpool.* Henry Young and Sons, 1953.

Picture Credits

The sources for the illustrations in this book are shown below. Credits from left to right are separated by semicolons, from top to bottom by dashes.
Cover: From the Collection of the Ulster Museum, Belfast. Front and back endpapers: Drawing by Peter McGinn.
Pages 6, 7: George F. Mobley, courtesy U.S. Capitol Historical Society. 9: Library of Congress. 10: Courtesy of the Mariners Museum, Newport News, Virginia. 12-15: Rare Book Division, The New York Public Library, Astor, Lenox and Tilden Foundations. 16, 17: Painting by Leslie Wilcox, photographed by Mark Sexton, courtesy The Pilgrim Hall, Plymouth, Massachusetts. 21: Pilgrim Society, Plymouth, Massachusetts. 22: Culver Pictures. 25: Peabody Museum of Salem. 27: John Carter Brown Library, Brown University. 29: National Portrait Gallery, Smithsonian Institution. 31: Virginia State Library, Richmond. 32-37: Courtesy of the Trustees of the British Museum, London. 38, 39: Maryland Historical Society. 40: Cooper-Bridgeman Library, courtesy Thomas Coram Foundation for Children, London. 42: Courtesy of the Council of the Dorset Natural History and Archaeological Society in the Dorset County Museum, Dorchester, England. 44: Courtesy of the Essex Institute, Salem, Massachusetts. 46: Library of Congress. 47: By courtesy of the Wellcome Trustees, London—Library of Congress. 48: Library of Congress. 49: Drawing by John Batchelor. 50, 51: Courtesy W. D. and H. O. Wills, Bristol, England. 52-55: Det Kongelige Bibliotek, Ms Ny Kgl Saml 565, Nummer 4. Tegninger og Samlinger til en Beskrivelse over de Salzburgske Emigranters Etablissement Ebenezer i Georgia. Copenhagen. 56: I. N.

Phelps Stokes collection, Art, Prints and Photographs Division, The New York Public Library, Astor, Lenox and Tilden Foundations. 57: Courtesy of the Mariners Museum, Newport News, Virginia. 58: Courtesy the Harvard University Portrait Collection, Gift of John Hancock. 59: Museum of Fine Arts, Boston. 60: Library of Congress. 62: The Rhode Island Historical Society. 63: Courtesy of the Boston Public Library, Print Room. 66, 67: Henry Beville, courtesy the Mariners Museum, Newport News, Virginia. 68-75: I. N. Phelps Stokes Collection, Prints Collection, The New York Public Library, Astor, Lenox and Tilden Foundations. 76, 77: Paulus Leeser, courtesy private collection. 78, 79: Library of Congress. 80, 81: Painting by John Stobart, photograph courtesy Kennedy Galleries. 83: Courtesy of the New-York Historical Society. 84, 85: The Metropolitan Museum of Art, Bequest of Edward W. C. Arnold, 1954. The Edward W. C. Arnold Collection of New York Prints, Maps and Pictures. 86: Al Freni, courtesy Philadelphia Maritime Museum. 87: Mark Sexton, courtesy Bostonian Society. 89: Painting by John Stobart, photograph courtesy of Kennedy Galleries. 91: Library of Congress. 94: Henry Groskinsky, courtesy Philadelphia Maritime Museum. 95: Henry Groskinsky, courtesy Philadelphia Maritime Museum, except center left, Al Freni, courtesy Philadelphia Maritime Museum. 97: Frontispiece, copper engraving by James Narine and Co. from Copy of the Last Will and Testament of Robert Richard Randall, Butler Library, Columbia University Libraries, courtesy Barnett Shepard. 98, 99: INA Corporation Museum. 100, 101: Peabody Museum of Salem. 102: Library of Congress. 104: Bettmann Archive. 106, 107: Derek Bayes, courtesy Mersey Docks and Harbour Company, Liverpool; Derek Bayes, courtesy National Maritime Museum, London. 108, 109: Derek Bayes, courtesy Liverpool City Libraries. 110: Derek Bayes, courtesy Liverpool City Libraries—Derek Bayes, courtesy Mersey Docks and Harbour Company, Liverpool. 111: Derek Bayes, courtesy Mersey Docks and Harbour Company, Liverpool. 112, 113: Hirschl and Adler Galleries. 115: Peabody Museum of Salem. 116: Library of Congress. 119: Courtesy of the New-York Historical Society. 121-123: Drawings by John Batchelor. 124: Al Freni, courtesy INA Corporation Museum. 125: Smithsonian Institution, Photo No. 80-1594. 126-128: Peabody Museum of Salem. 130-134: Library of Congress. 136-141: Drawings by Richard Schlecht. 142-144: Library of Congress. 145: Merseyside County Museum, Liverpool. 147, 149: Library of Congress. 150: Chicago Historical Society. 152: Colonial Office Papers, c.o. 384/92, Public Record Office, London. 153: Culver Pictures. 155-157: Library of Congress. 158, 159: Al Freni, courtesy J. Welles Henderson Collection. 160: Inset, courtesy of the British Museum, London, Peabody Museum of Salem. 161: Inset, Library of Congress, Peabody Museum of Salem. 162, 163: Museum of the City of New York. 165: Library of Congress. 167: Courtesy of the Mariners Museum, Newport News, Virginia. 169: The Metropolitan Museum of Art, The Alfred Stieglitz Collection, 1933.

Acknowledgments

The index for this book was prepared by Gale Linck Partoyan. The editors wish to thank the following: John Batchelor, artist, and Cedric Ridgely-Nevitt, consultant (pages 121-123); Peter McGinn, artist (endpaper maps); Richard Schlecht, artist, and William Avery Baker, consultant (pages 136-141).

The editors also wish to thank: In Canada: Wolfville, Nova Scotia—C. P. Wright. In Denmark: Copenhagen—Professor Sven Gissel, Manuscript Department, Det Kongelige Bibliotek; Kristian Hvidt, Parliament's Chief Librarian. In France: Paris—Marcel Redouté, Curator, Marjolaine Mathikine, Director for Historical Studies, Jacques Chantriot, Catherine Touny, Musée de la Marine; Chantal Chobeau, Musée S.N.E.I.T.A.; Blérancourt—Martine Diot, Musée National de la Coopération Franco-Américaine; Le Havre—André Malraux, Franck Duboc, Gaston Legoix, Musée des Beaux-Arts; Geneviève Testanière, Curator, Musée du Havre. In Germany: Hamburg—Dr. Jürgen Meyer, Altonaer Museum; Rolf Finck, Hapag-Lloyd. In Japan: Tokyo—Tsukasa Itoh, Fujita Kogyo and Mrs. Fusae Tajima. In the United Kingdom: London—R. Williams, Department of Prints and Drawings, The British Museum; Stephen Riley, Ships Department, Barbara Tomlinson, Picture Department, National Maritime Museum; Bertram Newbury, The Parker Gallery; Bristol—Hubert Rudman, Archivist, W. D. and H. O. Wills; Cornwall—Oliver Price, Honorary Curator, Falmouth Museum; Liverpool—Denise Roberts, Janet Smith, Liverpool City Libraries; R. R. Harvey, Senior Estate Assistant, Mersey Docks and Harbour Company. In Belfast, Northern Ireland—Eileen Black, Ulster Museum.

The editors also wish to thank: In the United States: Washington, D.C.—Kermit Roosevelt Jr., Kermit Roosevelt and Associates, Inc.; Jerry Kearns, Sam Daniel, Mary Ison, Annette Melville, Division of Prints and Photographs, Tom DeClaire, Gary Fitzpatrick, Reference Librarians, Geography and Map Division, Library of Congress; John Stobart, Maritime Heritage Prints; Robert Mawson, National Trust for Historic Preservation; James Knowles, Museum Specialist, Division of Transportation, National Museum of American History, Monroe H. Fabian, Associate Curator of Paintings and Sculpture, National Portrait Gallery, Smithsonian Institution; Florence C. Miller, Administrative Assistant, U.S. Capitol Historical Society; Annandale, Virginia—Caroline Sigrist; Baltimore, Maryland—Charles Hughes; Erik Kvalsvik, Paula Velthuys, The Maryland Historical Society; Bath, Maine—Nathan Lipfert, Curator, The Maine Maritime Museum; Boston—Mary Shannon, Boston Arts Commission; Stephen Nonack, Reference Librarian, The Boston Atheneum; R. Eugene Zepp, Print Department, Boston Public Library; Thomas Parker, Director, Mary Leen, Librarian, The Bostonian Society; John Cushing, Librarian, Miss Collins, Librarian, Russell Urquhart, Library, The Massachusetts Historical Society; Alex Chandler, Museum of Transportation; David Dearborn, Curator, New England Historic Genealogical Society; Professor W. M. Fowler, History Department, Northeastern University; William Osgood, Brenda Jackson, State Street Bank and Trust Company; Robert C. Vose, The Vose Gallery; Carbondale, Illinois—Professor Donald Adams, Department of Economics, Southern Illinois University; Charleston, South Carolina—Captain Robert Bennett, Commanding Officer, Marine Safety Office, U.S. Coast Guard; Chicago, Illinois—Trudy Hansen, Assistant Curator, Graphics Collection, Chicago Historical Society; Crofton, Maryland—Glen Berger; East Boston, Massachusetts—Ciro Giordano, East Boston Community Development Corporation; East Hampton, New York—Dorothy T. King, Head Librarian, The Long Island Collection, East Hampton Free Library; Lincoln, Massachusetts—Francis H. Gleason; Mobile, Alabama—David Toenes, Mobile Chamber of Commerce; Mystic, Connecticut—Richard C. Malley, Assistant Registrar, Mystic Seaport Museum; New Bedford, Massachusetts—Paul Cyr, Librarian, Genealogical Room, New Bedford Free Library; Elton Hall, New Bedford Whaling Museum; New London, Connecticut—Paul Johnson, Librarian, United States Coast Guard Academy Library; New York, New York—Mrs. M. P. Naud, Hirschl and Adler Galleries; Barbara Shikler, Librarian, New York Historical Society; Gretchen Wessels; Newport News, Virginia—Larry D. Gilmore, Assistant Curator, Paul Hensley, Archivist, John O. Sands, Assistant Director for Collections, Lois Oglesby, Curatorial Assistant, The Mariners Museum; Philadelphia, Pennsylvania—Joseph Welles Henderson; Debra J.

Force, Curator, The Insurance Company of North America Corporation Museum; Philip C. F. Smith, Curator, Jeffrey Groff, Registrar, Philadelphia Maritime Museum; Plymouth, Massachusetts—Anne Harding, The General Society of Mayflower Descendants; Laurence R. Pizer, Director, Jeanne M. Mills, Curator of Manuscripts and Books, Pilgrim Society; James Baker, Librarian, Plimoth Plantation; Providence, Rhode Island—Richard B. Harrington, Curator, The Anne S. K. Brown Military Collection; C. Danial Elliott, Bibliographical Assistant, The John Carter Brown Library; Maureen Taylor, Graphics Curator, Rhode Island Historical Society Library; Richmond, Virginia—Dr. Louis H. Manarin, State Archivist, Archives and Records

Division, Virginia State Library, Commonwealth of Virginia; Salem, Massachusetts—Marylou Birchmore, Administrative Assistant, Essex Institute; A. Paul Winfisky, Assistant Curator of Maritime History, Mark Sexton, Photographer, Kathy Flynn, Photographic Assistant, Peabody Museum; Savannah, Georgia—Mills Lane, The Beehive Press; Sea Level, North Carolina—Captain Leo Krazewski, Sailors Snug Harbor; Staten Island, New York—Captain Sherwood Patrick, Captain Richard S. Rouche, United New York and New Jersey Flynn Sandy Hook Pilot's Benevolent Association; Williamsburg, Virginia—Parke S. Rouse Jr., Executive Director, Avril L. Switzer, Assistant Director, Walter K. Heyer, Director of Interpretation, Jeffrey J.

Geyer, Exhibit Interpreter, Jamestown Festival Park, The Jamestown-Yorktown Foundation; Woolwich, Maine—Mr. and Mrs. Thomas Gardiner; Worcester, Massachusetts—Mrs. G. Bumgardner, Curator of Prints, George Joyce, Library, American Antiquarian Society.

Particularly valuable sources of quotations were *The Great Migration: The Atlantic Crossing by Sailing-ship Since 1770* by Edwin Guillet, University of Toronto Press, 1963; *Redburn: His First Voyage* by Herman Melville, edited by Harrison Hayford, Hershel Parker and Thomas Tanselle, Northwestern University Press and the Newberry Library, 1969; and *From the Forecastle to the Cabin* by Captain S. Samuels, Harper & Brothers, 1887.

Index

Printed in U.S.A.

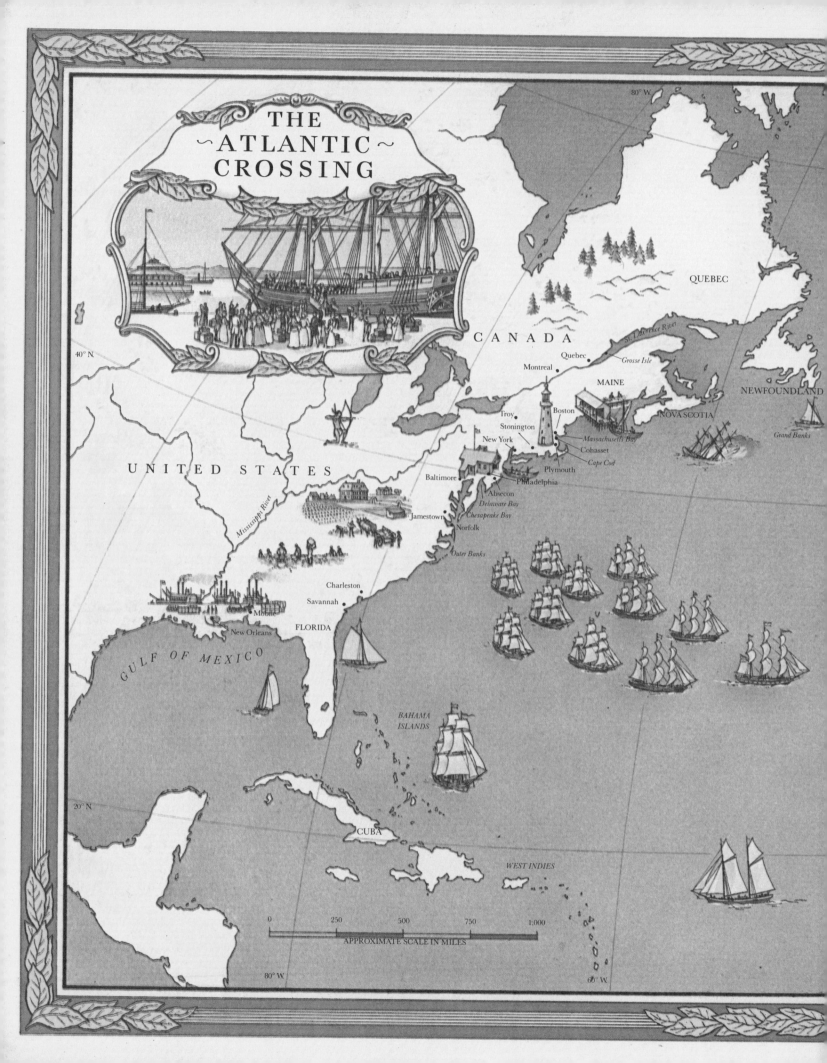

THE ~ATLANTIC~ CROSSING

80° W.

QUEBEC

CANADA

St. Lawrence River

Quebec

Montreal   Grosse Isle

MAINE

NEWFOUNDLAND

40° N.

Troy

Stonington   Boston

New York   Massachusetts Bay

NOVA SCOTIA

Cohasset

Grand Banks

Cape Cod

Plymouth

UNITED STATES

Baltimore

Philadelphia

Absecon

Delaware Bay

Mississippi River

Jamestown   Chesapeake Bay

Norfolk

Outer Banks

Charleston

Savannah

Mobile

New Orleans   FLORIDA

GULF OF MEXICO

BAHAMA
ISLANDS

20° N.

CUBA

WEST INDIES

0   250   500   750   1,000

APPROXIMATE SCALE IN MILES

80° W.   66° W.